For all the old-time music makers who added a little joy to the often isolated and somber homesteads of the Southern Appalachian Mountains.

Other books by John Rice Irwin:
The Arnwine Cabin
Baskets and Basketmakers in Southern Appalachia
Guns and Gunmaking Tools of Southern Appalachia
The Story of Marcellus Moss Rice and his Big Valley Kinsmen

When I asked my cousin, Horney Rodgers, several years ago how he rated himself as a fiddler, he paused for a moment and replied, "I'm the only man that I ever heard that played the fiddle jest exactly the way I wanted to hear it played." He is shown here on one of his visits to the Museum -- on the front porch of the Bunch cabin. Horney, who has been a farmer, a miller, and who has engaged in other mountain "enterprises", has several old fiddles, but plays only for his own amusement. He, like so many other musicians, is from neighboring Union County. (Photo by Wallace Denny)

Table of Contents

I	Foreword	7
II	The People and Their Music	9
III	The Fiddle	13
IV	The Mountain Banjo	31
V	The Mouth Bow	59
VI	The Appalachian Dulcimer	64
VII	Miscellaneous Instruments of Southern Appalachia (Guitar, Mandolin, Jews Harp, Harmonica, Etc.)	83
VIII	Addendum	92
	Index	103

Shown above are some of the instruments in the permanent display at the Museum of Appalachia. Each instrument is numbered and has a corresponding number in a booklet so that one may read the history of the instrument as he views it. (Photo by Pat and Bill Miller)

FOREWORD

For almost a quarter century I have gathered musical instruments (along with other items) from the hollows and mountains of Southern Appalachia, primarily in upper east Tennessee, southwest Virginia, western North Carolina and eastern Kentucky. These items are now on display at the Museum of Appalachia, fifteen miles north of Knoxville, Tennessee.

Scholars and other interested parties from throughout the country have suggested that photographs of these instruments, along with descriptive notes, be made available for those interested in conducting substantive research in this field; hence, the purpose of this short, simple treatise.

I have not attempted to conduct comprehensive or exhaustive examinations of any facet of the subject. It is, rather, an endeavor on my part to discuss briefly the various types of musical instruments found in Southern Appalachia; and to set down as many facts as possible relative to the specific instruments in the collection. I think it is important to know the maker of the instrument, its approximate age, the area of its origin, etc. My records, unfortunately, are often incomplete, or lacking altogether; but I am recording what information I do have before it is lost altogether. It is hoped that these bits and pieces will be used by future researchers (who possess more competency and time than I) to develop a truer picture and an historical documentation of the role music has played in the lives of the colorful people of the southern mountains, and subsequently the direct role played by these people in influencing music throughout the world.

J.R.I.

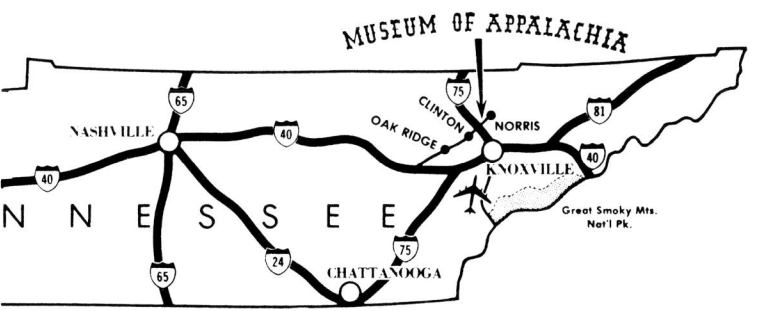

Shown here is a typical Sunday afternoon gathering of local musicians at the Museum of Appalachia. At the left is my cousin and next door neighbor, Carlock Stooksbury, playing the Jews Harp; Carl Bean of Mountain Road, who has been writing and singing songs since he was a lad; "Happy Jack" Rogers of Corryton, who started playing his grandfather's fiddle when he was six years old; the writer at the microphone playing the harmonica; Ted Wyrick from Tater Valley near the village of Luttrell (home of Chet Atkins), playing guitar; and the locally well-known Bob Cox who has been "fiddlin' nearly all my life." (photo by Wallace Denny)

The People and Their Music

Music has always played an important part in the lives of the people of this Appalachian region. Even in the most remote mountain cabin, shy of furniture and cooking utensils, one often finds two or three musical instruments. They valued their music and they took it quite seriously, although they may never have played outside the confines of their homes.

This attitude is illustrated by the following anecdote. My longtime friend, Jacob, one of twenty-six children, was talking to me in his tiny three-room house in confidential tones while his wife was out back chopping wood. Jake played the fiddle a little for himself, his brothers, and his neighbors. He had a cow and a garden and otherwise just loafed around while his wife worked in town. And in the most serious manner he looked over his glasses at me and said, "the old woman complains to me because I don't keep the firewood cut, but every time I start choppin' wood my hands git stiff and sore and hit makes it hard fer me to play the fiddle".

And so Jake sat in a broken down old chair before the fire and patted his big foot as he wailed out an old tune called "Cumberland Gap" on the fiddle. And as he did so, we could hear the ringing of the axe as his good wife buried it deep in the green hickory outside in the cold.

Within a few miles of this area there have been dozens of nationally known entertainers. Roy Acuff, the "King of Country Music," and Chet Atkins, the world's best known guitar player, were reared a few miles up the road in neighboring Union County. The world famous opera singer, Grace Moore, was from nearby Jellico, and the internationally renowned Mary Costa is from Knoxville. Others who were either from the Knoxville area, or who got their start there are Dolly Parton, Archie Campbell, Larry McNeeley, Carl Smith, Lois Johnson, Jack Greene, Carl and Pearl Butler, Tennessee Ernie Ford, Flatt and Scruggs, Kitty Wells, Johnnie and Jack, Homer and Jethro, Bill Carlisle and dozens of others.

I recall Dolly Parton on an early morning show for Knoxville groceryman Cas Walker when she was a mere child. She was one of many would-be stars from the surrounding area who would arise at 4 o'clock in the morning to be on "Cas Walker's program". I read recently accounts (with front page pictures) of Dolly following President Carter in an appearance in New York City's City Hall and drawing a substantially larger crowd than did the President. And Mayor Ed Koch gave her the key to the city.

This county (Anderson) has also made notable contributions with its early mountain-country musicians. My old friend, the late Hugh Cross, for example, had tremendous influence nationally on the course country music was to take. Known as Hugh Ballad Cross, he was one of the first to record country music in New York in the early 1920's. He worked with the legendary blind guitar player and singer Riley Puckett, the Skillet Lickers and others. He played with and became lifelong friends with Gene Autry, Roy Rogers and turned down a chance to go to Hollywood. His friend Gene Autry accepted.

It was Hugh who rewrote, and lengthened the "Wabash Cannonball" and he was one of the first to record it. He became well-known as a performer on the WLS Barn Dance in Chicago, and later he became Master of Ceremonies of the Boone County Jamboree over WLW in Cincinnati. He wrote many songs, some of which were recorded by the popular national bands of the day. Some of his songs contributed to the rise and fame of such notables as Roy Acuff, Bill Monroe, etc. Among the numerous songs are: "I Traced Her Little Footprints in the Snow" and "Don't Make Me Go To Bed and I'll Be Good".

Hugh, who was from the nearby town of Oliver Springs, was typical of the early musicians of this region. He was carefree, happy, and eternally optimistic; and although he had gained national fame, worked with some of the country's best known personalities, and made lots of money, his last days were spent in near destitution.

He had suffered two fires in which he lost all his memorabilia. He had sold the rights, I understand, to most of his songs, and he had lost one of his legs. He lived with relatives in Oliver Springs, and owned one cheap guitar; but he was one of the most unselfish men I have ever known. He was selling some sort of mail-order goods, but he seemed to have given away more items than he sold. We occasionally had him as our guest for supper, and he never failed to bring my wife "some little present" as a token of his appreciaton.

I talked with Hugh the day before he died and I remember vividly his laughing about his illness, stating he knew he had only a few days and adding, "I've had enough fun for a hundred men -- it ain't bothering me none."

Hugh's time, like so many of those who were pioneers in the country-bluegrass field, had passed him by long before his death. Few of his neighbors, and practically no one in this county remembered the legendary Hugh Ballad Cross of earlier fame when he died in the late 1960's. Yet millions of people around the world could hum or were familiar with a half dozen of his songs.

Lester McFarland, also from the hamlet of Oliver Springs, teamed up with Bob Gardner and they became famous as "Mac and Bob." These two blind singers recorded almost a hundred songs during the 20's and 30's on the Vocalion and Brunswick labels. They gained even more popularity on the WLS Barn Dance.

Fiddlin' Bill Seivers and his family, who lived in Clinton, seven miles from the Museum, became popular in the late 1920's. According to Charles K. Wolfe in his well-researched book, **Tennessee Strings,** Bill's daughter, Willie, was the first woman in country music to achieve fame as an instrumentalist. "She won national recognition as a champion guitarist," Wolfe points out. Willie still performs with her brother, Mack, of nearby Clinton. Fiddlin' Bill, his son Mack, daughter Willie, and Walter McKinnie started playing locally in 1925 and were known as the "Tennessee Ramblers". Mack, who is my long-time friend, states that they started recording for Brunswick, and eventually made personal appearances in towns from the Great Lakes to the Gulf of Mexico. Many years later, after the passing of Fiddlin' Bill and McKinnie, Mack and Willie changed their style and formed a group called the "Novelty Hawaiians" which is still a popular local group.

Another famous string band was formed in the early twenties by my old friend, "Fiddlin' " Jimmy McCarroll of adjoining Roane County. This band, which recorded for Columbia, was known as the "Roane County Ramblers", and they gained the most renown in the late twenties and early thirties.

I first met Uncle Jimmy about 1965 in the little rented log cabin where he lived in a remote section of Roane County. And although his group had long since disbanded and he was quite old, he was still a great fiddler, banjo picker, and guitar player. Uncle Jimmy learned to play the fiddle, he stated many times, from his grandmother who was part Cherokee.

The extent to which this small region has contributed to and influenced the music of the country is legend. Whether one speaks of country, folk, traditional mountain, or bluegrass, he can gain much insight into the historical development of "his" music by studying these crude antecedent instruments, and by familiarizing himself with the colorful people who made and played them.

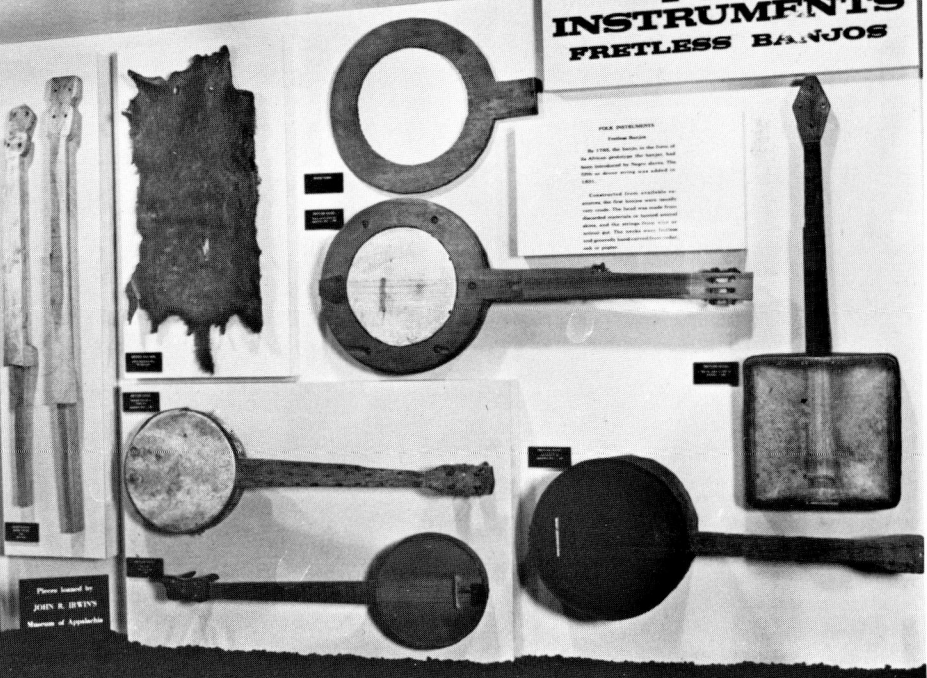

Shown here are a few of the Museum of Appalachia folk instruments on temporary loan to the Country Music Hall of Fame in Nashville.

Fiddlin' Bob Cox, left, joins Carlock Stooksbury, shown here playing the Jews Harp, on a Sunday afternoon at the Museum. My father, Glenn Irwin, enjoyed the old tune so much that he stopped his whittling, temporarily, to listen.

Both Bob and Carlock were "raised" on the mountain road, two miles south of the Museum. Bob had chances to go with the famous Bill Monroe band (the father of bluegrass) many years ago; but he preferred to stay at home to care for his aging father in their log cabin home at the foot of Blueberry Ridge. (Photo by the author).

The Fiddle

The fiddle, in my opinion, has been the most universally accepted instrument in the mountains. It was as equally treasured in the mansions of the few wealthy landowners as it was in the one-room dirt-floored mountain cabin; and it has had a profound influence on all types of music which had its origin in this region.

The Grand Ole Opry is the longest continuous radio program in America and one of the most popular. Numerous television shows have sprung from it; over ten million people have viewed it live; and its impact on country, western, bluegrass music, etc. is world wide.

When the Opry opened on November 28, 1925, it was Uncle Jimmy Thompson, a native of Smith County, Tennessee who played his fiddle throughout the entire program. As a matter of fact, Judge George D. Hay, the man who founded the Opry, was inspired to start the legendary program after attending an old-time fiddlin' session in a remote log cabin. Fiddlin' John Carson of Fannin County, Georgia, is generally recognized as being the first country music recording star, and Bob Taylor, Tennessee's fiddlin' governor, is credited for discovering Carson.

The history of the fiddle, as we know it, goes back to the 1600's in Europe where the master violin makers in Italy (and later Germany) pretty much perfected the instrument. The instruments made by the old mountain fiddle makers, those made by Stradivari, Amati and Paganini of Italy, and the factory made instruments of today look almost identical to the lay person. Musical quality, however, varies greatly, as does the price -- from $10.00 to a quarter of a million dollars.

Some of the early settlers brought with them fiddles that their ancestors carried from Europe; but many who came across the Smokies carried only a rifle, an axe, and a few household items necessary to survive in the wilderness, and the fiddle was not often among those possessions.

During the first two or three generations on the frontier most families had little time for entertainment of any sort and much less the time to make a conventional instrument. There were, however, some improvised fiddles made of gourds, and later of old cigar boxes, etc. The period during the latter part of the 1800's, and in the early twentieth century, seemed to have produced more interest in this art.

Surprisingly, there were few so-called fiddle makers in the mountains. In all my travels I have found only a half dozen. Many, and perhaps most of the early mountain homes had no musical instrument at all; and when they did acquire one, it was often made by some member of the family. The fiddle is probably the most difficult of all instruments to make, and that is why it took a man with special skills. On the other hand, almost anyone could make a playable banjo. Although I have found more homemade banjos in Appalachia than fiddles, I have never heard of an old "banjo maker" -- an indication that most families made their own.

I asked Charles R. Moore, my lawyer friend from nearby Maynardville, about the fiddle makers he had known. Charles was reared in rural Union County (one of Tennessee's smallest) and he is one of the most astute and perceptive observers of our local history and culture I know. He interrupted his county law practice for a career in Washington; and at the time of his retirement there, he was Regional Director of the Federal Trade Commission and in that capacity had charge of all the Commission's field offices in the country. He then returned to the village of Maynardville and resumed his law practice, farming, and visiting with the folk of the area. The following is his account of the only two recognized fiddle makers Union County has produced as far as we know. But this tiny county produced such notable musicians as Roy Acuff, Chet Atkins, Carl Smith, Lois Johnson, dozens of other lesser known professional musicians, and thousands of good "back porch" fiddlers, pickers, and singers.

A relatively small number of our mountain folk in this area have gained recognition as makers of fine violins. However, two old-time fiddlers in Union

County, A.L. Cassady and Evart Acuff, made violins that local fiddlers consider excellent instruments.

When Mr. Cassady (called Uncle Fate in his latter years), returned from the Civil War, where he served in the Union Army that made the famous march from Atlanta to the Sea, he acquired a farm in Beard Valley, six miles south of Maynardville, in Union County, and opened a blacksmith shop where he demonstrated unusual skills in working with metals and woods. He was of Southern Irish descent and a typical Irishman in appearance, temperament and wit.

Fate thought the fiddles commonly in use in this area were not very good and upon one occasion he was criticizing their quality to some of his fiddling friends; they suggested that he try his hand at making a better one. He accepted the challenge and about the year 1885 began studying the fiddles owned by his friends and also the limited literature he could acquire relative to the art of violin making. He took old fiddles apart to get a better idea as to their physical construction. There were no fiddle makers among his acquaintance to teach him the art.

Fate began gathering and seasoning woods employed in making fiddles, such as blue poplar for fingerboards; curley or birdseye maple for backs, sides, necks and bridges; spruce for the front; dogwood for the pegs, tail pieces and end pins; and pine for linings, sound posts and bar. While these woods were seasoning, he devised and made various carving tools and clamps for use in shaping the parts of the violin and holding them in place while being glued together. He used burnt umber and other dark stains in finishing the violins which did not do justice to the fine woods he used.

Mr. Cassady eventually was given a good pension for his military service and this enabled him to spend less time farming and smithing and to devote more time to fiddle making. He usually made one or two fiddles each year. He gave several of his fiddles to old fiddling friends; others, he sold at low prices, such as twenty-five to seventy-five dollars. These fiddles are still highly prized by local musicians for their excellent tone. Fate said each fiddle had a personality.

Uncle Fate's son, Richard, became a lawyer, blacksmith, and a fine fiddler, but to Uncle Fate's disappointment, he never became interested in fiddle making.

Evart Acuff, son of Charles B. Acuff, the best violinist around Maynardville, and cousin of the now world-famous Roy Acuff, was a rural mail carrier and went by Uncle Fate's home and shop daily. In those days rural roads were in very poor condition and could be traversed only on horseback or with a one-horse sulky, and a few miles' travel could exhaust man and beast. Evart enjoyed stopping at Uncle Fate's shop and getting a drink from the huge spring that flowed from a cave near the blacksmith shop. And, occasionally, also a wee drink of moonshine whiskey. He became intrigued with Mr. Cassady's personality and skills and made many inquiries as to how the various operations in fiddle making were performed.

In 1922, Uncle Fate told Evart that his age was taking its toll on his skills and that if Evart was interested, he would not only teach him how to make violins but would give his tools and woods to him. Evart readily accepted the offer. So, he gave Evart the tools and woods with the admonition, 'D--- you, Evart, don't ye loan these tools; they'll git away from ye and by that time I'll be gone and there'll be no one left to make ye another set.'' Evart became a very apt pupil and by 1923 had made a pretty good fiddle, which Uncle Fate complimented.

Before his death in 1973, at the age of 81 years, Mr. Acuff had completed thirty-six violins. His skills increased and his violins improved in quality as he gained experience. Evart experimented with and successfully used apple and wild cherry woods for the backs, necks and sides of his violins. The cherry finished quite beautifully. He used an oil varnish which he believed materially improved the tone of his violins.

Mr. Acuff's violins began selling at a very low price but at the time of his death he had sold several violins for several hundred dollars each and two that he had just finished he had priced at one thousand dollars and two thousand dollars, respectively. Since Uncle Fate's time, good fiddles and a good fiddler had come to be greatly appreciated.

Evart Acuff gave one of his violins to his famous cousin, Roy Acuff, who has played it often on his Grand Ole Opry program in Nashville. It was a great source of satisfaction for Evart to see one of his fiddles played by such a renowned musician.

Due mainly to the fervor developed by the great revivals in the early 1800's and later in camp meetings, the fiddle was often considered to be the "devil's instrument" and there is an old mountain expression, "as thick as fiddlers in hell." As a small boy I was mildly admonished for my own attempts at playing the fiddle, and as a result started playing old hymns. This prompted a relative to declare that the fiddle was never intended as an instrument for religious music.

The names of the old fiddle tunes often reflect the light and sometimes frivolous nature of the music. Some examples are: "Hell Among the Yearlings"; "Devil's Dream"; "Sally Goodin"; "Long Eared Mule", "Whistlin' Rufus"; "Soppin' the Gravy'"; "Dog in the Rye Straw", "Did You Ever See The Devil, Uncle Joe?", etc.

There seems to be a revival of the fiddle in popularity today with the development of bluegrass and with the large number of bluegrass festivals, fiddlers' conventions, etc. I think it fair to say that the fiddle is the most difficult of all stringed instruments to master--and in this writer's opinion, its music is the most beautiful.

While the fiddle was often associated with the lazy and the trifling, this was not always the case. The many fiddling contests often included some of the more prominent men of the community. My great uncle, Lee Irwin, who won fiddlin' contests throughout East Tennessee, was held in high esteem. As a child I recall viewing him as a great hero, because everyone extolled his musical capabilities, most exclaiming that "Lee Irwin is the best fiddler that I ever heard". Though he was a very old man when I was a child, I recall the slow, carefully noted tunes he played; "The Merry Widow's Waltz", "Bonaparte's Retreat", "The Gray Eagle", "Billy in the Low Ground", etc.

As the following illustrations indicate, and as stated earlier, there is little obvious variation in the style and construction of the fiddle. But some of those made in this region were crude, and even pathetic, attempts at recreating the instrument perfected by the early masters.

Charles Gene Horner, one of only two known living fiddle makers in all East Tennessee, is shown here in his little shop on the Cumberland Plateau near the community of Westel, in Cumberland County, Tennessee. When he was fifteen years old he heard some old time fiddle players in nearby Crossville, the county seat, and he was so impressed that "I decided right then and there that I wanted to devote my life to fiddlin' and to fiddle making," and he has done just that. After serving a hitch in the army and later "working for the government a short while" he started spending full time "on my music".

He became a first class country fiddler (he has his own band) and he became a true master fiddle maker. Now he supports his family in the small shop which sits beside the tiny log house where he was reared. He has made over a hundred fiddles and several mandolins and banjos for Grand Ole Opry stars as well as for local "Saturday night" fiddlers. Musicians tell me that his instruments are of the highest quality. "I'm doin' just exactly what I've always wanted to do", Gene decided as he sat whittlin' on a fiddle neck in his cluttered little workshop. (Photo by Steve Jernigan)

Gene Horner, left, points out to the writer the fine quality curly maple back on one of his recently completed fiddles. "A lot of people think you have to get your wood from Europe," Horner explains, "but this maple growed here on the mountain, and you can see how it turned out. Both fiddles shown here were made by Horner. (Photo by Steve Jernigan)

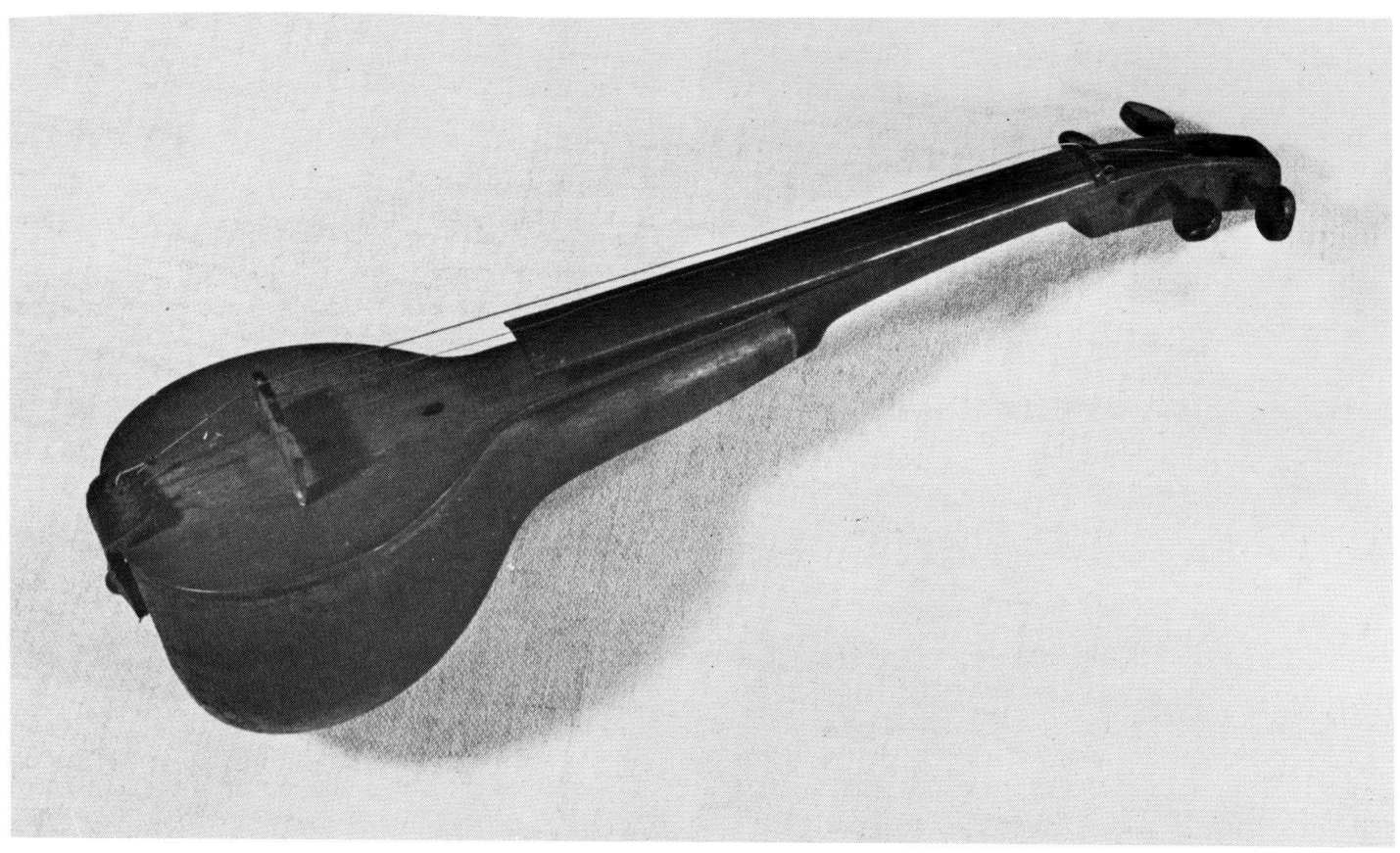

GOURD FIDDLE

I had heard that some of the early pioneers, characteristic of their resourcefulness and ingenuity, made fiddles from gourds; but I had never seen one. When my friend, Carl Bean, told me of one he saw in the little fiddle maker's shop in the mountains of Cumberland County, I investigated immediately.

The shop belonged to Gene Horner, possibly the best old-time mountain violin maker in the state. But the gourd fiddle belonged to one Andy Parky who lived over in Roane County. After several unsuccessful attempts, I finally located Andy, and to my surprise found that he was a native of Hancock County, Tennesee, my favorite area for finding pioneer-type artifacts.

This fiddle was made, Andy told me, by his great uncle Frank Couch who lived in Mill House Hollow, which is near the Mulberry community in Hancock County, Tennessee, near Lee County, Virginia. Couch made the fiddle as a young man, about 1840. The last known fiddler to play this instrument was the locally famous George McCarroll of Roane County. Although I was not able to buy the fiddle from Andy, he insisted that I "take it and keep it fer people to see how the old people had to do". (Photo by Pat and Bill Miller)

Tom Cassady, grandson of fiddle maker Fate Cassady, is shown here examining a fiddle made and signed by his grandfather which is on display at the Museum. Tom, who is a noted fiddler himself, still lives on his grandfather's homeplace at Beard Road, Union County, Tennessee. (Photo by the author)

FATE CASSADY FIDDLE

This fiddle was made in 1910 by A.L. (Fate) Cassady, shown above, who lived in Union County, a few miles east of the Museum. Cassady was one of the best known fiddle makers in this area and was responsible for teaching this art to Evart Acuff, Roy's first cousin, himself a noted instrument maker. The Cassady fiddles are considered to be exceptionally fine instruments and are quite rare even in this area. It is signed as follows: "made by A.L. Cassady, 1919". (Photo of Cassady courtesy of Lance Cassady)

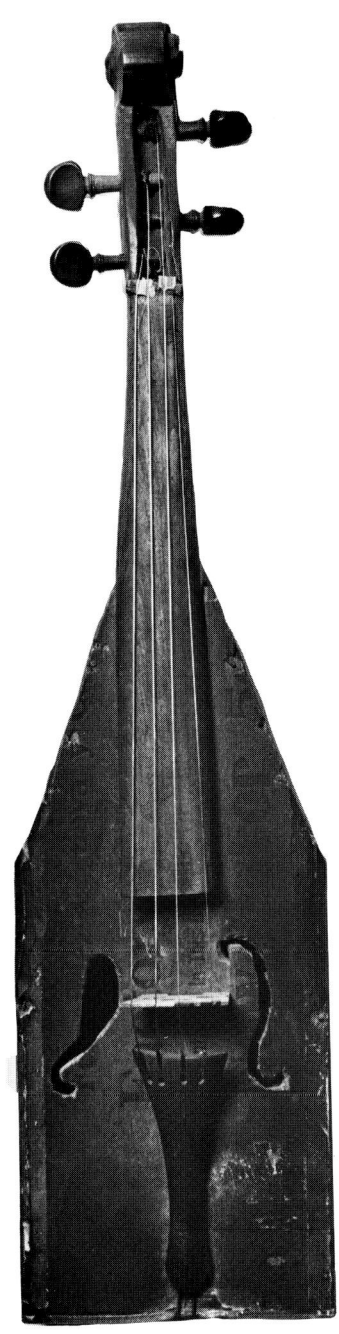

CIGAR BOX FIDDLE

This fiddle was made in the early days of the depression by the late Luther Hill in a small mountain community in Union County, Tennessee. The body is of an old wooden cigar box and the neck is hand carved. Hill, who wrote poetry for his own amusement, was also a school teacher. The fiddle, which has a remarkably good tone in relation to its appearance, was acquired from Hill's daughter, Mrs. Florence Allred, of Sevierville. It is now on loan to the Country Music Hall of Fame in Nashville. (Photo by Dana Thomas.)

CRUDE FIDDLE CASE

This is easily the crudest fiddle case I have seen. The two sides and the large end are made of one rived four inch wide piece of hickory, bent to accommodate the curvature of the top and bottom pieces. It was acquired from that Cumberland Mountain area. (Photo by Pat and Bill Miller)

WALNUT FIDDLE CASE

This fully dove-tailed, all walnut case is the most unusual one I have seen; and the hasp is a fine example of graceful blacksmith work. The case and fiddle came from the historic village of Fort Blackmore, Virginia, about a hundred miles "up Clinch River" from the Museum. (Fort Blackmore was the "jumping off" point for parties going down the Clinch to Nashville and to other wilderness areas.)

The case, according to information from Guy Bowers from whom I bought it, was made in 1847. The fiddle inside is unsigned, but is an old one, showing much wear on the neck. (Photos by Pat and Bill Miller)

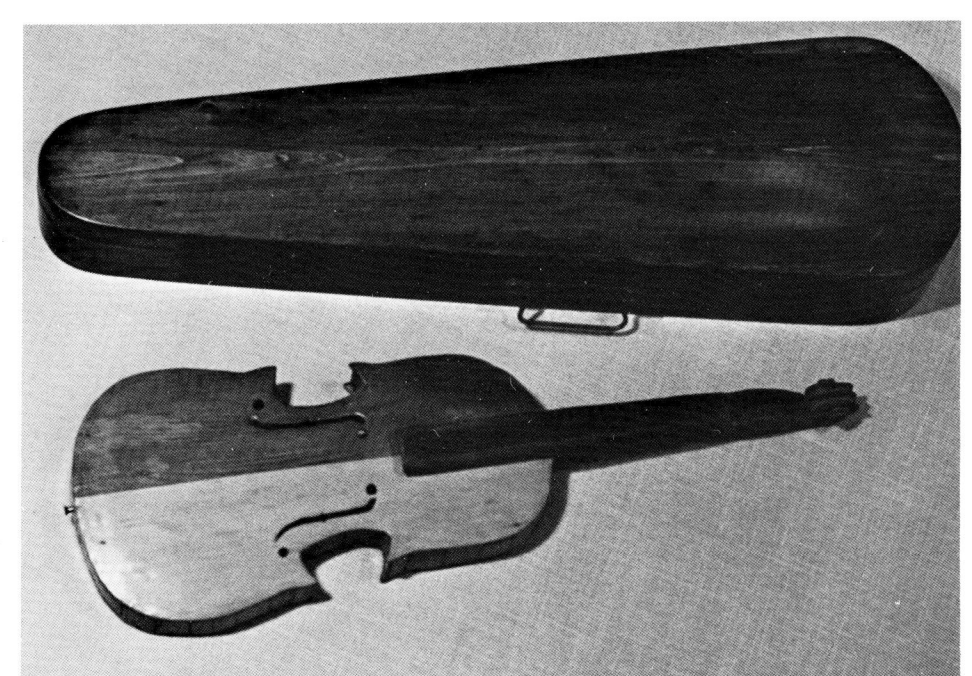

CRUDE MOUNTAIN FIDDLE

This is one of the poorest fiddles in terms of workmanship, style, form, and quality I have seen. Although it is a local piece, I do not know the name of the maker -- and if I did, I would not divulge it. The case is the common coffin-shaped type. (Photo by Pat and Bill Miller)

STAINER FIDDLE

The Stainer is one of the rarest and most valuable of the German-made violins. Whether or not this signed instrument is an original or an old copy, I do not know. I purchased it from Charlie Kinch of Jonesboro, the state's oldest town. He acquired it from an old home nearby. There were many early German settlers in that upper East Tennessee region. As a matter of fact, the name "Stainer" or "Stiner" is a common name in this area, the family having settled quite early in Union and Campbell counties. (Photo by Pat and Bill Miller)

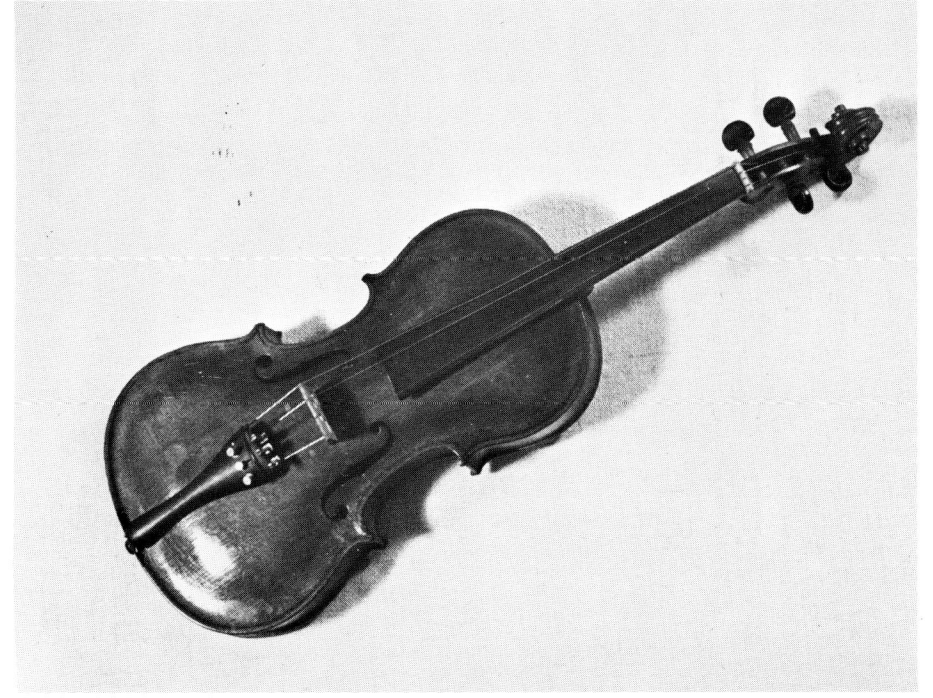

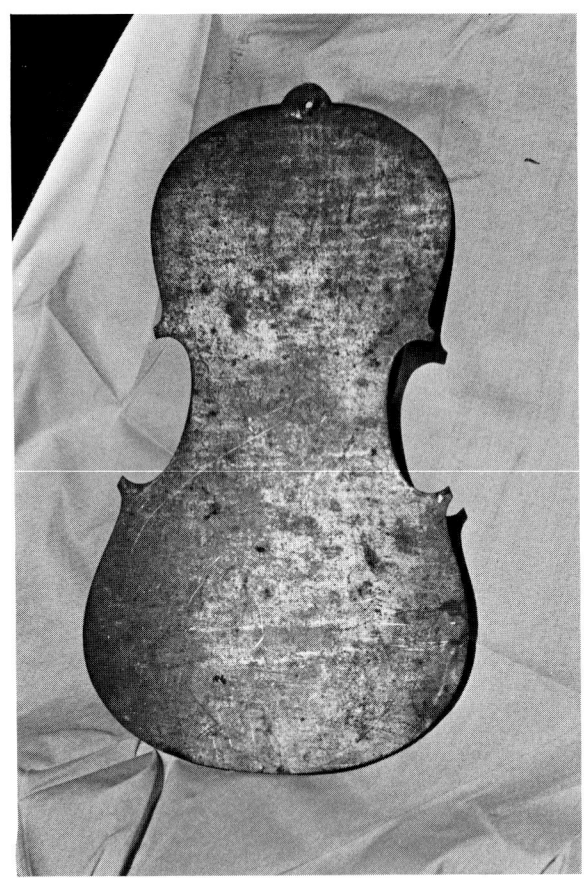  

FIDDLE PATTERNS AND FORMS

The early tin pattern, left, and the well-made form shown in the center were obviously made by a master violin maker. I acquired them from the late Guy Bowers of Greeneville, Tennessee, about 1970. He bought them in "the old Dutch settlement" of Greene County in the thirties. The crude form at right, from the hills of Claiborne County, Tennessee, is obviously a self-styled one -- not a copy of the classic style. (Photo by Steve Jernigan)

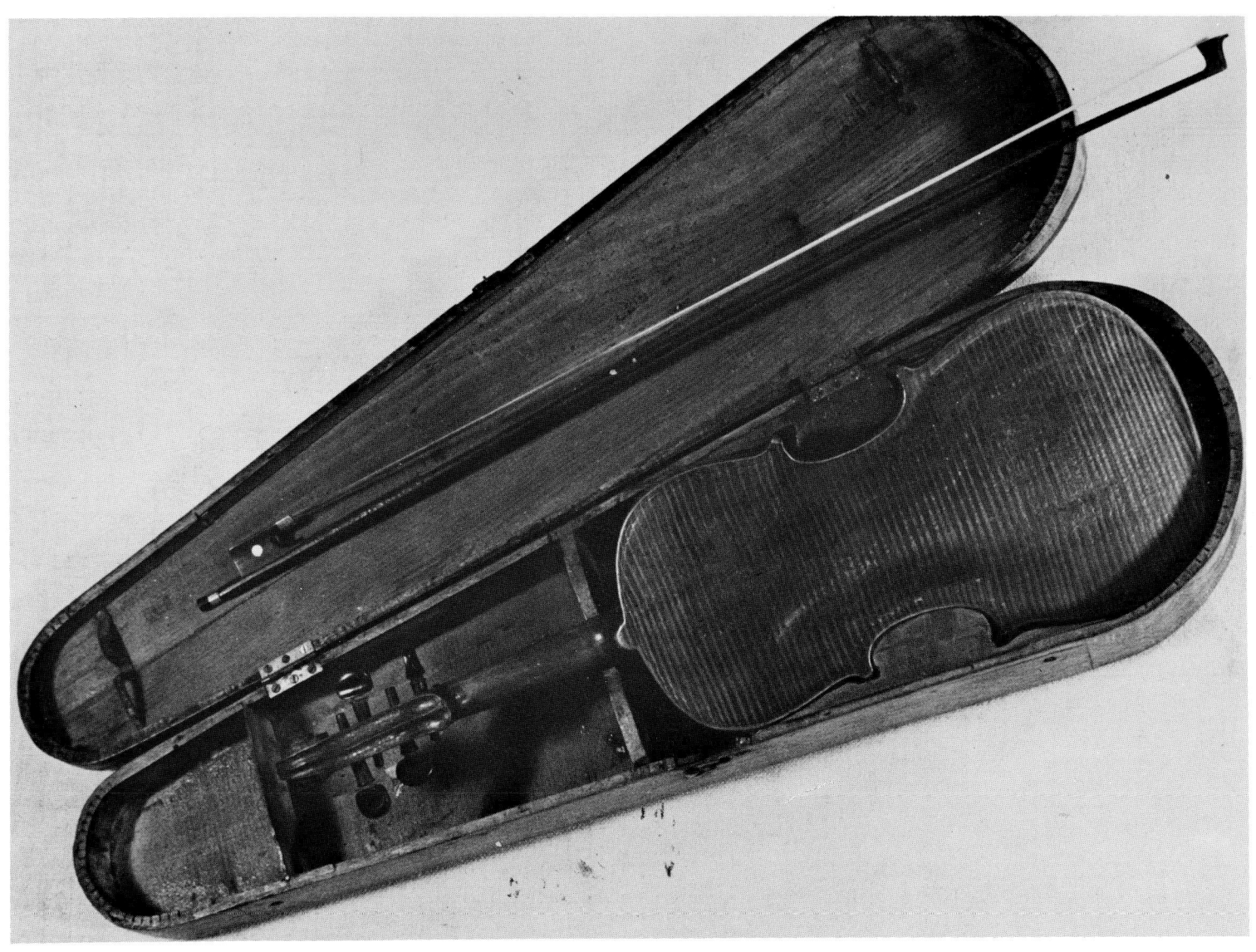

McLAIN FIDDLE

This unsigned country-made fiddle has the most pronounced curly maple back I have seen. It came from the old McLain homeplace near Baileytown in Hawkins County, Tennessee, and is said to have been made by John McLain. It was acquired from David Byrd of Erwin, Tennessee, who bought it from the McLain family. It is a well-made instrument, and I should think one of good musical quality. (Photo by Pat and Bill Miller)

WORTH McCOY FIDDLE

Worth McCoy, who for many years lived across the road from the Museum, made this fiddle for his own use. Although it is shaped similar to the classical violins, it is very heavy, and void of inlay which is found on almost all such instruments. Worth, who is now (1979) well into his nineties, made this instrument of red cedar in 1958. It is the only instrument I have seen made of cedar, and I doubt that it has any appreciable musical qualities. (Photo by Wallace Denny)

"NEW STYLE" FIDDLE

This instrument reflects another unsuccessful attempt to improve the aesthetic and musical qualities of the ancient style and form of the fiddle. Acquired in East Tennessee, its maker is unknown. (Photo courtesy of Dana Thomas)

Clyde Cox, one of the two fiddle makers I know of in this entire region, is shown here with an instrument he has just completed. Clyde, who lives in the nearby community of Karns in Knox County, learned the art when a young man from a neighbor, old Harrison Kelley, who had taught himself how to make fiddles "at the wood pile". He has made 81 fiddles; and although he is a perfectionist and spends many months in the completion of a single instrument, interestingly, he has never attempted to sell his fine products and has almost all of the ones he has completed in the 42 years since he started. They are displayed in a little shop near his home. He does, however, have each instrument priced, ranging from $200 to $1500. Clyde's ancestors settled near where he now lives soon after the Revolutionary War. In addition to the Cox family, he is related to the Leinarts, Smiths and Gallahars, all early settlers in that area. (Photo by Steve Jernigan)

STILLMAN LAMBERT FIDDLES

These crude instruments were made by Stillman Lambert of Bowden, W. Virginia. After he retired from his life's work of logging and timber cutting, he, recalling his father's fiddling and his own involvement with a banjo as a lad, decided to make himself a fiddle. He wasn't able to readily acquire a conventional fiddle to use as a pattern; so he "jest made up my own pattern." He said, "I first made it in my head."

Born near Bowden in 1894, Lambert thinks he has made about 100 of these instruments. "Until recently, I never sold any -- jest give them to my relatives. Then I sold them to first one then another."

Lambert recalls a cheap old fiddle his father used to play which "come unglued ever time it rained." To prevent such occurrences in his fiddles, Lambert "glued on the top and the back, and then I nailed them, and that way I'm shore the damn things'll never come off."

These fiddles, the fretless banjo shown in the photograph and the accompanying form which are now on display at the Museum, were purchased from Lambert by Roddy Moore of Ferrum, Virginia, mentioned earlier. It was from Moore that I acquired them. (Photo by Pat and Bill Miller)

← MINIATURE FIDDLE

This small fiddle was doubtless made as a "curiosity" rather than to be played. I bought it from Bob Johnson of Rossville, Georgia, operator of the museum, "Whistle in the Woods". (Photo by Pat and Bill Miller)

HAND CARVED FIDDLE →

Although this crude instrument is evidently Appalachian made, it has the ornate carving on the end of the peg box reminiscent of European violins. Acquired from my friend Carl Bean, this instrument came originally from the East Tennessee area. (Photo by Pat and Bill Miller)

HIRAM SHARP FIDDLES

When old Hiram Sharp (1885-1976) of nearby Scott County, Tennessee, wanted a fiddle to play, he made it from 'scratch', just as he made the banjo and mouth bows he played. He also made the fiddle bow, using horse hair to string it. The instrument at left is made of wood, using the conventional pattern. The one above, however, is made of metal, the only fiddle I have seen of this type.

The Sharps in this area were of German origin and established Sharp's Fort near here in 1784. In addition to his music endeavors, Hiram was a farmer, logger, clock and gun repairman, etc. He made a pair of tooth pullers and served as the local dentist; he used herbs for medicine and was the unofficial doctor of the community. He had his own barber shop (and even a barber chair which is now in the Museum) and he made coffins and served as the local undertaker, even learning to embalm bodies. His son Don remembers that his father was kept very busy during the flu epidemic of 1919 making coffins for those who died in the community. He lived in a remote section of Scott County, Tennessee, near the village of Norma. The mountain county of Scott is the home of Congressman John Duncan and U.S. Senator Howard Baker. This instrument is now on loan to the Children's Museum in Oak Ridge. (Photo at left by Alan Halbert) (Photo by Steve Jernigan)

FIDDLENECKS

These four fiddlenecks, along with the fiddle bow, shown at left, were made by old Hiram Sharp of Scott County, Tennessee, discussed earlier. The o'possum hide at right apparently was being processed to use as a banjo head.

CELLO-FIDDLE?

This unusual instrument may be classified as an oversized, rectangular shaped fiddle, but because of its large size it may also be termed a type of cello. It was purchased from Nancy Walton of Knox County who acquired it from my trader friend, Rowe Martin, of near Limestone in upper East Tennessee, the birthplace of Davy Crockett. Rowe acquired it near Jonesboro, the state's oldest town. The floral folk-art designs are similar to the designs on some dulcimers and to those found on some furniture in this area. (Photo by Pat and Bill Miller)

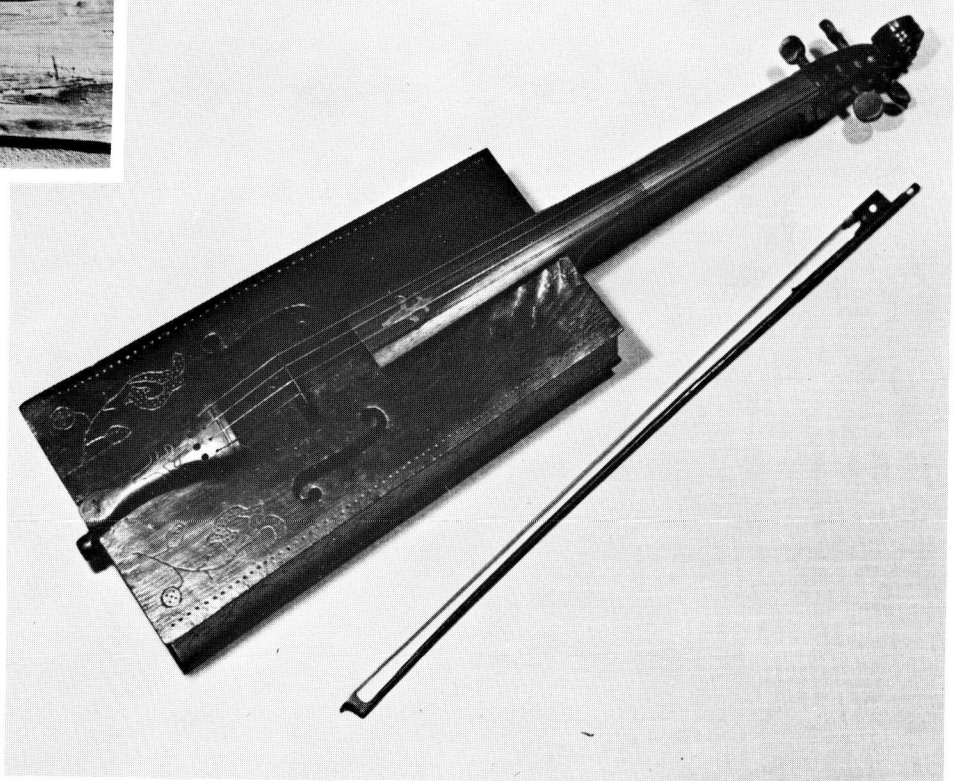

Shown here is the original "Tennessee Ramblers" band formed by Fiddlin' Bill Sievers who lived just six miles south of the Museum in Clinton. Pictured with Bill on the left is his daughter, Willie, with the banjo, his son, Mack, and Jerry Taylor with the mandolin. This picture was taken in front of the house where, according to Mack, his sister was living at the time. She, according to the noted authority, Charles Wolfe, became "one of the first women in country music to achieve fame as an instrumentalist...". After the death of Fiddlin' Bill, Mack, with the help of Willie, formed a band he called "The Novelty Hawaiians" which is still quite active in the East Tennessee area. (Photo courtesy of Mack Sievers)

Fiddlin' Bill Sievers of the nearby town of Clinton organized the original Tennessee Ramblers band in 1929. He, along with his son Mack and daughter Willie, became well-known throughout this area and played with some of the best-known country music people of the day. (Photo courtesy of Mack Sievers)

THE MOUNTAIN BANJO

The statement is often made that the banjo is the only musical instrument indigenous to America. Those who have researched the banjo seem to agree that the now famous five-string banjo, as we know it, originated in America, but the extent to which the forerunner of this instrument was developed in other countries is not clear.

What appears to have been the ancestor of our modern banjo was made of gourd with horse hair strings and was found in the West Indies in the 1600's and in Africa. This form of the instrument was apparently brought into this country by the Black slaves.

Tradition has it, and later researchers seem to agree, that a Blue Ridge Mountain boy, from near Appomattox, Virginia, fashioned the first five string banjo. Joel Walker Sweeney, born in 1810, worked on his father's farm along with the family slaves. He learned their tunes and started playing the fiddle with them at their quarters after the day's work. It was, ostensibly, from one of their crude rhythm instruments that Joel got the idea for a "banjar". He reportedly added a sound box and a fifth string. He and his two brothers found appreciative audiences around the courthouse in Appomattox, and they started making appearances in the area. Their local fame spread, and they soon were performing in surrounding states. By 1841 they were touring the country with their minstrel-type act, and soon thereafter they toured Europe, and played for Queen Victoria.

The homemade banjo, which the Sweeney brothers did so much to popularize, was soon to be manufactured by several American firms. But the mountain folk of this region were not accustomed to store-bought items, and the banjo was no exception.

I have found many unusual instruments, possessing varied shapes, some of solid wood, some of metal, some with skin heads, etc. But virtually all of the crude and unusual instruments I have found have one common characteristic: they have four strings, and the all important fifth string, or thumb string -- always shorter than the other four. Hence it qualifies, as far as my categorization is concerned, as a banjo.

Some of the old mountain men I have known referred to the instrument as a "banjar". The late John Carrico who lived a few miles east of the village of Fort Blackmore, Virginia, and who had played with the early Carter family, also spoke of the banjar, with a strong accent on the first syllable. (He owned one of the oldest fretless banjos I have seen.) Interestingly, Thomas Jefferson in his *Notes on Virginia* spelled it b-a-n-j-a-r apparently because of the manner in which he had heard it pronounced.

Possibly the most popular banjo player of all time was the famous Uncle Dave Macon of Smart Station near McMinnville, Tennessee. He was called "The Dixie Dew Drop", "King of the Hillbillies", etc. As a child, I recall the neighbors congregating around the few battery operated radios in our community to listen to "Uncle Dave" on the Saturday night Grand Ole Opry.

The old method of playing the banjo involved the use of only the thumb and forefinger, a technique that has gained great popularity in recent years. The now famous "three finger roll" style of playing was popularized largely by Earl Scruggs of North Carolina, but who started his career in nearby Knoxville. When Scruggs joined up with Bill Monroe, and "His Blue Grass Boys" of Kentucky, it wasn't long before that type of music was called "Bluegrass".

So the five-string banjo, which was developed in Virginia, became universally popular as a homemade instrument in the Southern Mountains in the latter part of nineteenth and the early part of the twentieth century, suddenly was revived in the 1950's. The extent to which the banjo was responsible for the rapid and phenomenal growth of bluegrass music has undoubtedly been great. And the popularity of the modern bluegrass banjo is due largely to Earl Scruggs and others from the mountain area, and the old-time mountain banjo players who used crude instruments as are displayed in this exhibit.

Renda Whitaker is shown here with the banjo she and her husband made soon after they "started housekeeping" on the Cumberland Plateau at Lick Skillet, near Monterey, Tennessee. "We went to the woods and we cut us a poplar sapling. Then we killed us a ground hog, to make a head and we made us a banjo."

This instrument has been loaned temporarily by the Museum of Appalachia to the Country Music Hall of Fame in Nashville. (Photo by the author)

Levi Collins, who lives some twelve miles northwest of the Museum in Cherry Bottom (near Lake City, Tennessee) has worked as a miner, farmer, and miller since he was a child. He also plays the five string banjo, "the old fashioned way" by using the thumb and forefinger -- a technique now referred to as the "claw-hammer" style. Levi was "raised" across Pine Mountain from my childhood home in a most remote place called Bear Creek Hollow. The government purchased this area when Oak Ridge was built, and the most sensitive atomic plants were built there on Bear Creek. (Photo by Wallace Denny)

CRACKER'S NECK BANJO

This banjo came from a very old log cabin in Grainger County in a narrow hollow called Cracker's Neck. The house was built by the Idol Family who were prominent early German settlers in that region. The banjo was made, I am told, by "old Arthur Welch" who lived back in the mountains. It is one of the few completely handmade banjos I have seen -- there not being a single factory made piece about it. The head is made of groundhog hide, and the band is made of hand-rived hickory sawed at intervals on the inner side so as to provide for bending the timber into a circular shape. The brackets are of wire. I purchased it from the Coffman family who owned the cabin as well as the banjo. (Photos by Pat and Bill Miller)

BANJO NECKS

These fretless banjo necks from different old homeplaces in Appalachia were the labor of some would-be banjo makers who never got around to finishing their respective instruments. (Photo by Pat & Bill Miller)

GROUNDHOG HIDE USED FOR MAKING BANJO HEADS

The hide was tanned by burying it in the ground for three days in wood ashes. Large squirrel and cat hides were also used for making banjo heads, but groundhog was preferred. This one was skinned and tanned by Charlie Blevins of near Robbins in Scott County, Tennessee. (Photo by Pat and Bill Miller)

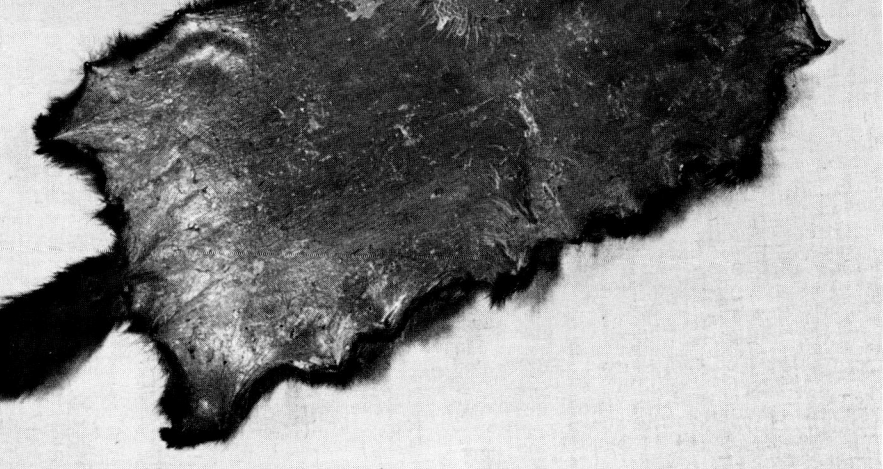

ROANE COUNTY BANJO

One of the crudest mountain banjos I have found, this one has the skin head (believed to be made of cat hide) which is merely tacked onto the wooden rim. It is the only banjo I have seen which had no brackets whatever. The neck, though crudely made, is of walnut. It comes from neighboring Roane County, Tennessee. (Photo by Pat and Bill Miller)

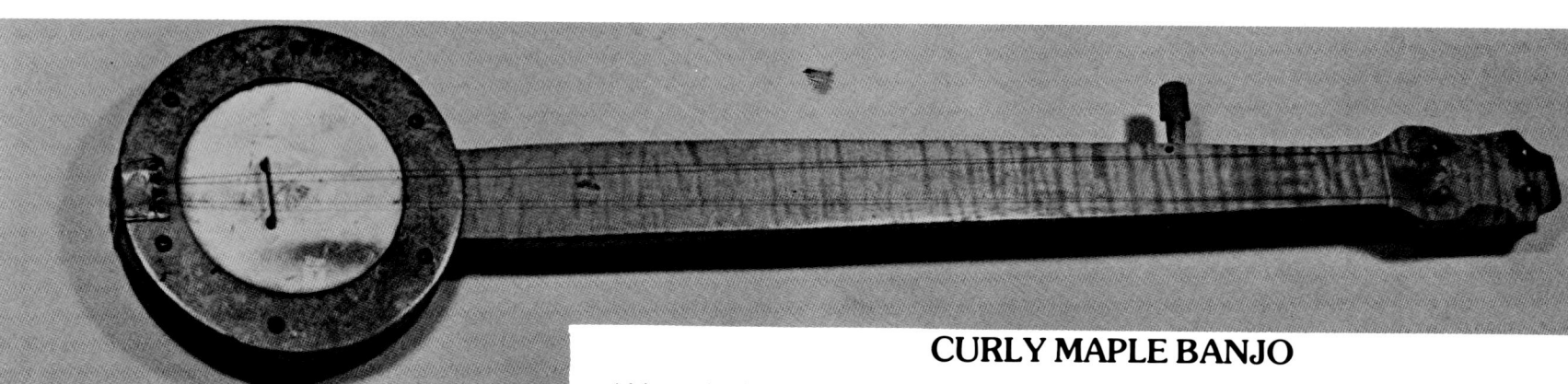

CURLY MAPLE BANJO

Although this fretless banjo has a home-tanned groundhog hide for the head, and otherwise is of an old style, it is of later vintage than many instruments in the collection. It has a large wooden rim and a small head that I have found only in the area in and around th Great Smoky Mountains. This one was made in western North Carolina and is of curly maple, and was purchased from Mark King of Blountville. He acquired it in Wataga Co., N.C. at White Top Mountain, where he has found others of this type. (Photo by Pat and Bill Miller)

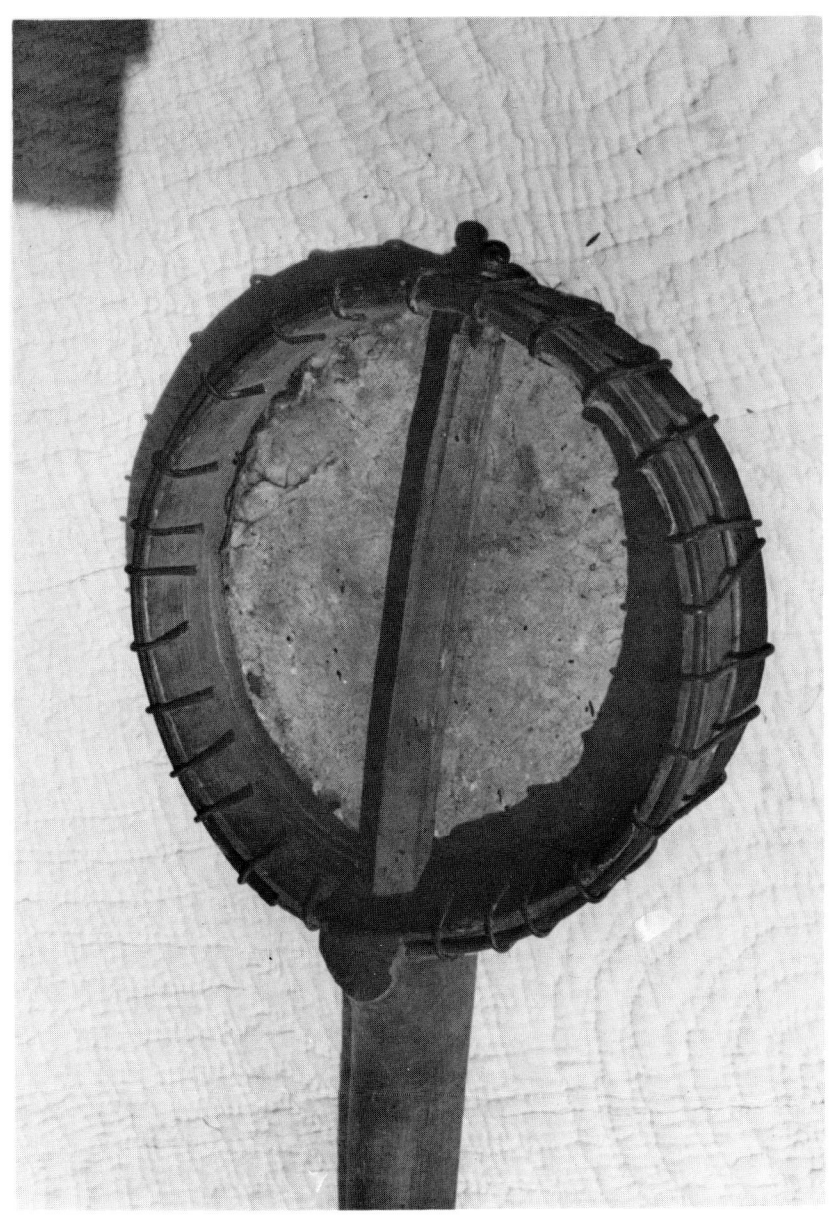
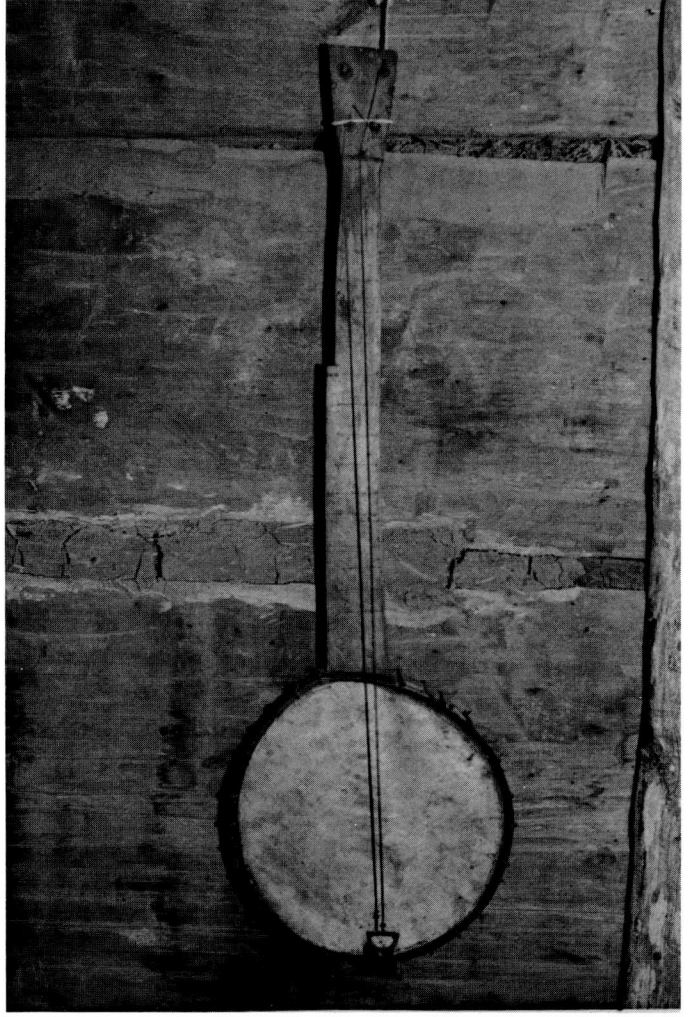

ROANE COUNTY BANJO

This classic example of the crudely made Appalachian banjo came from the Cumberland Mountain section of Roane County, a few miles west of Harriman. The rim is of rived white oak, the brackets of heavy wire, and the head of ground hog skin. Although it is a fretless instrument, the spacing of the frets is marked. (Photo by Pat and Bill Miller)

RUFUS GRAVES BANJO **LUTHER GRAVES**

Rufus Graves of neighboring Union County was a farmer and a Baptist preacher as well as the father of twenty-six children -- thirteen by each of his two wives. In his olden days he gave this banjo to his oldest son, Scott, who apparently took it "up north" when he went there to work in his younger days. On the under side of the head is written: "1926 #1629 N. Morris St. Scott Graves, KoKoMo, Indiana".

The Graves family was one of the earliest to settle in this valley -- in the late 1700's. I knew Rufus' second wife and many of the twenty-six children. During my early childhood many of them lived near my Grandfather Rice's place on Bull Run Creek in northern Knox County, Tennessee. In later years, when Scott got too old to play the banjo, it fell into the possession of his brother Grant from whom I acquired it.

Luther Graves and most of his 25 brothers and sisters learned to play the banjo from their father Rufus. Luther is shown here playing his "bicentennial" banjo on the porch of his Bull Run Creek home in neighboring Knox County. (Photo by the author)

Shown here is Grant Graves of adjoining Knox County, Tennessee, from whom the Graves banjo was purchased. This picture was taken in 1976 when Grant was 84 years old. (Photo by Pat and Bill Miller)

ONE PIECE BANJO

This crude mountain instrument can be characterized as a banjo only because it has five strings and because the fifth one is shorter and is not intended to be noted. Both the body and the neck are made of a single piece of pine. It was acquired about 1968 from Mary Ellen Walker of Morristown who acquired it in the foothills of the Great Smoky Mountains. (Photo by Pat and Bill Miller)

OCTAGONAL BANJO

This eight-sided, five-string banjo has an all wood constructed body. I purchased it from Mary Ellen Walker of Morristown, Tennessee, who acquired it from that upper East Tennessee area. It is one of only two instruments of this type I have seen, and I have no knowledge of its origin. (Photo by Wallace Denny)

HARRY LEE OLLIS BANJO

This is one of two wide-rimmed, small-headed banjos of this type I have found. It bears the name "Harry Lee Ollis" of Marion, North Carolina, who I assume to be the owner, and perhaps the maker as well. The neck is maple, the thick rim is of walnut, and the head is of a partially-tanned groundhog skin, expertly replaced by my neighbor, Bob Crowell of Norris. (Photo by Dana Thomas)

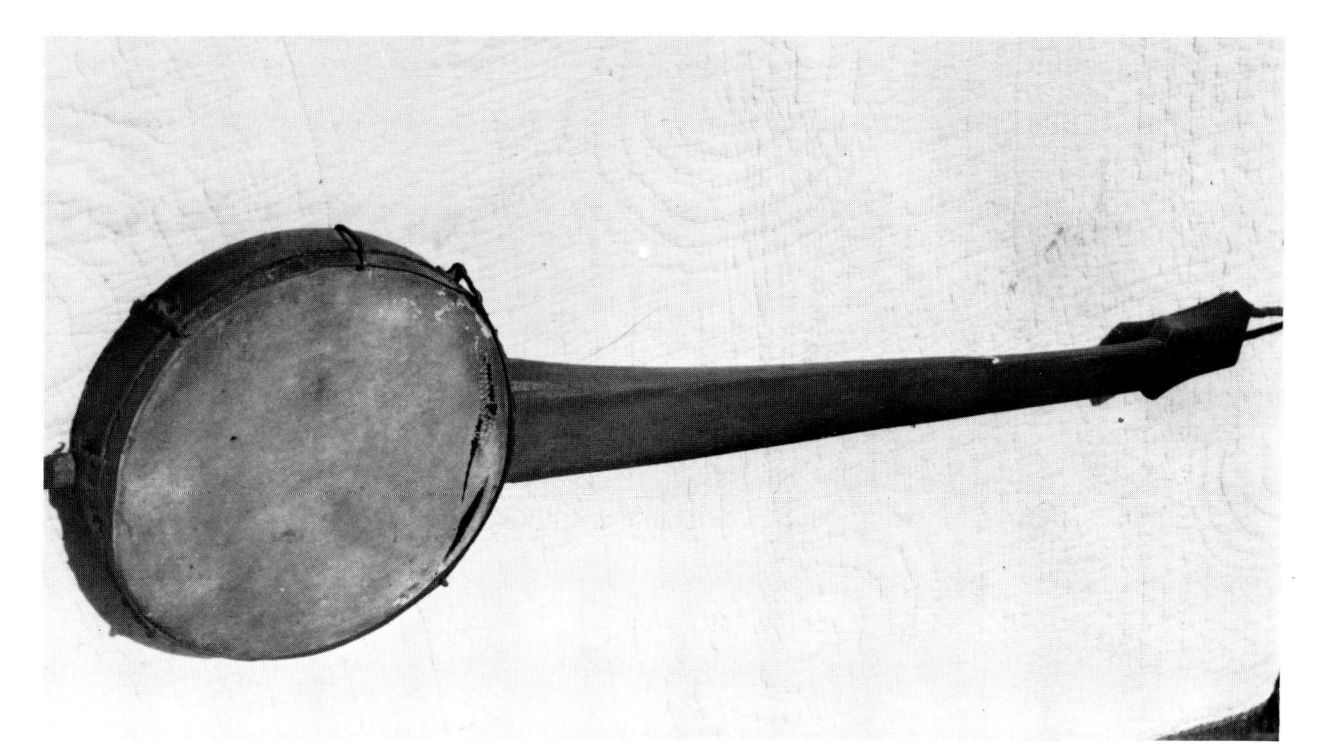

UNION COUNTY BANJO

This plain, simple five string banjo came from near Maynardville in adjoining Union County, where so many of the early country music greats originated. It is fretless and has only six brackets. (Photo by Wallace Denny)

HAM CAN BANJO

When my friend, Dow Pugh of near Monterey, Tennessee, in Putnam County, decided that he wanted a banjo, in typical mountain fashion, he made himself one from the materials available -- and the Selecto ham can served as the body. Dow became one of the South's better known woodcarvers, and over 200 pieces of his work are on display in the folk art area on the second floor of the display building here at the Museum of Appalachia. (Photo by Wallace Denny)

Dow Pugh, who lives on the Cumberland Mountain near Monterey, in Putnam County, Tennessee, is shown in his home among many of his creations. He made the ham can banjo shown above. (Photo by Wallace Denny)

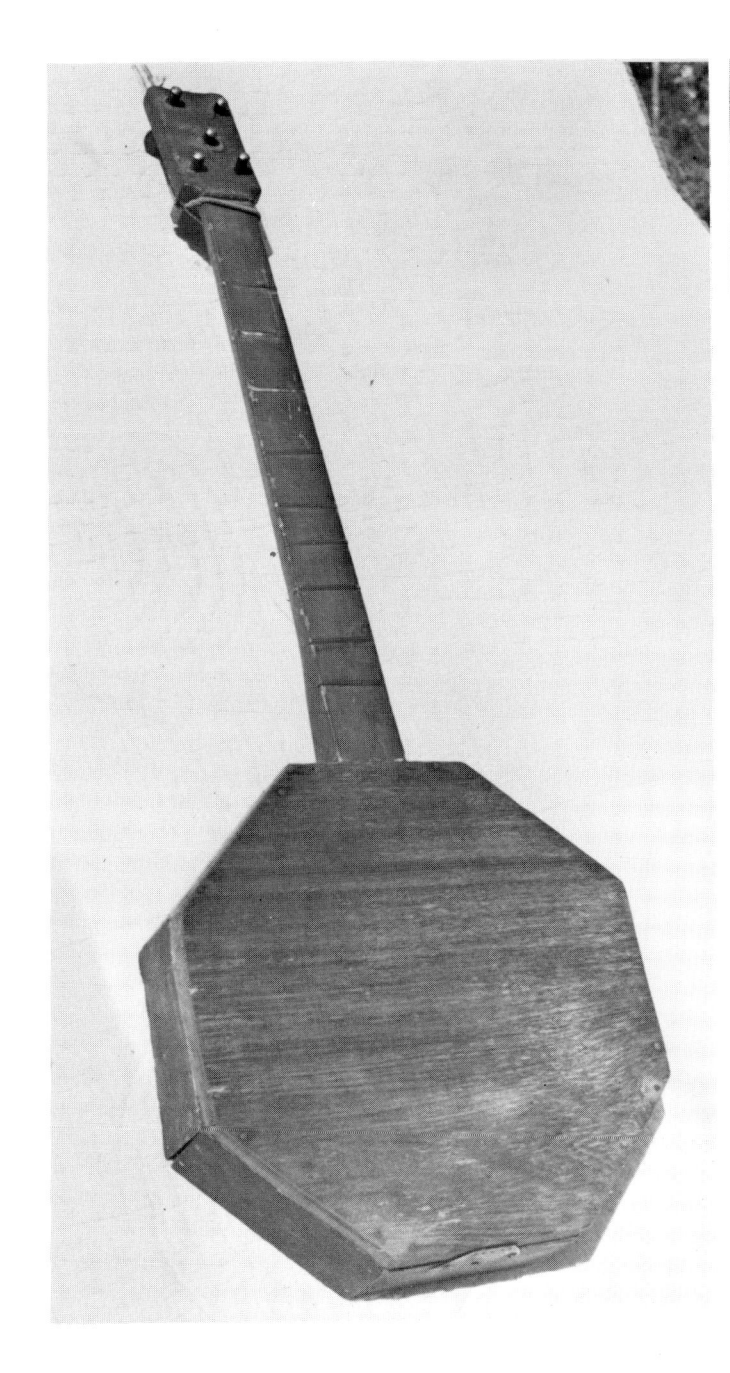

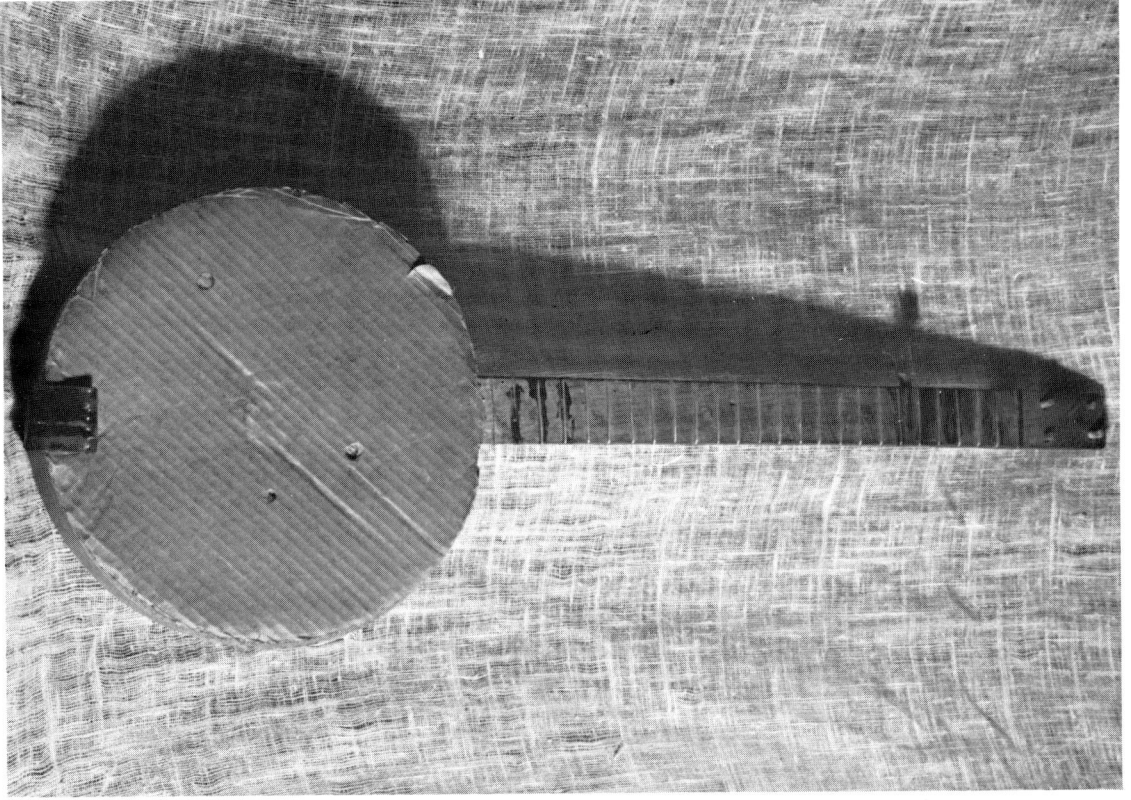

CARDBOARD BANJO

One of the characteristics of the "old timers" was that they "made do" with what they had. Someone spent many hours carving the neck, inserting the frets, etc. and then used a piece of cardboard for the head. This banjo is from Knox County, Tennessee, though its maker is unknown. (Photo by Alan Halbert)

CLAIBORNE COUNTY OCTAGONAL BANJO

Although I classify this instrument as a banjo because of its obvious similar characteristics, it does not have the customary short fifth string. It is the only "banjo" I have seen with all five strings extending the entire length of the neck. The arrangement of the keys is also unique. This banjo was purchased from Lee Hill of Tazewell in Claiborne County, some thirty-five miles east of the Museum. (Photo by the author)

Tater Hole Joe Johnson, called the hermit of Marlow, had few possessions other than his banjo, and I seldom visited him when he did not have it by his side. The following short account of his passing was written by the well-known columnist Bert Vincent in the "Knoxville News Sentinel".

Tater Hole Joe Johnson is dead. That maybe doesn't mean much to you because you didn't know him. I knew Tater Hole, and I spent many a pleasant hour with him sitting outside the hole in the ground, which was his home, listening to him singing and picking his banjo and telling tall tales, mountain tales, hant tales and just tales.

His hole, his home, was near Marlow, Dutch Valley, Anderson County. The hole had been dug and used to store Irish potatoes during winter months. It was maybe eight feet deep, and 10 by 12 in dimension. It was covered over, or roofed, with timbers, and the timbers overlaid with dirt. It was warm in winter, and cool in summer. He had a cook stove, a bed, a chair, a table and a lamp. He had worked for the Southern Railway, and I understand was living on a pension.

He didn't need much money because he didn't ask much from life --just a few friends, his banjo, his songs, his stories, and his memories.

Tater built a little cabin on top of the ground near his hole, and had lived in it during the last few years. He was 84 years old. (Photo 1963 by the author)

SQUARE-HEADED BANJO

This instrument, according to the inscription inside, was made by Allen Syck of Pike County, Kentucky, in 1928. The neck is of oak, and the head is of groundhog hide, the only such square-headed instrument I have seen. It was acquired by this Museum from Professor Roddy Moore of Ferrum College in Virginia and is now on loan to the Country Music Hall of Fame in Nashville. **(Photo by Dana Thomas)**

CLAIBORNE COUNTY BANJO

The rim of this banjo is of heavy birdseye maple, and the head is groundhog hide, apparently a replacement of the original. It was purchased from my long-time friend, Lee Hill of Tazewell, who bought it in his native Claiborne County, Tennessee. (Photo by Wallace Denny)

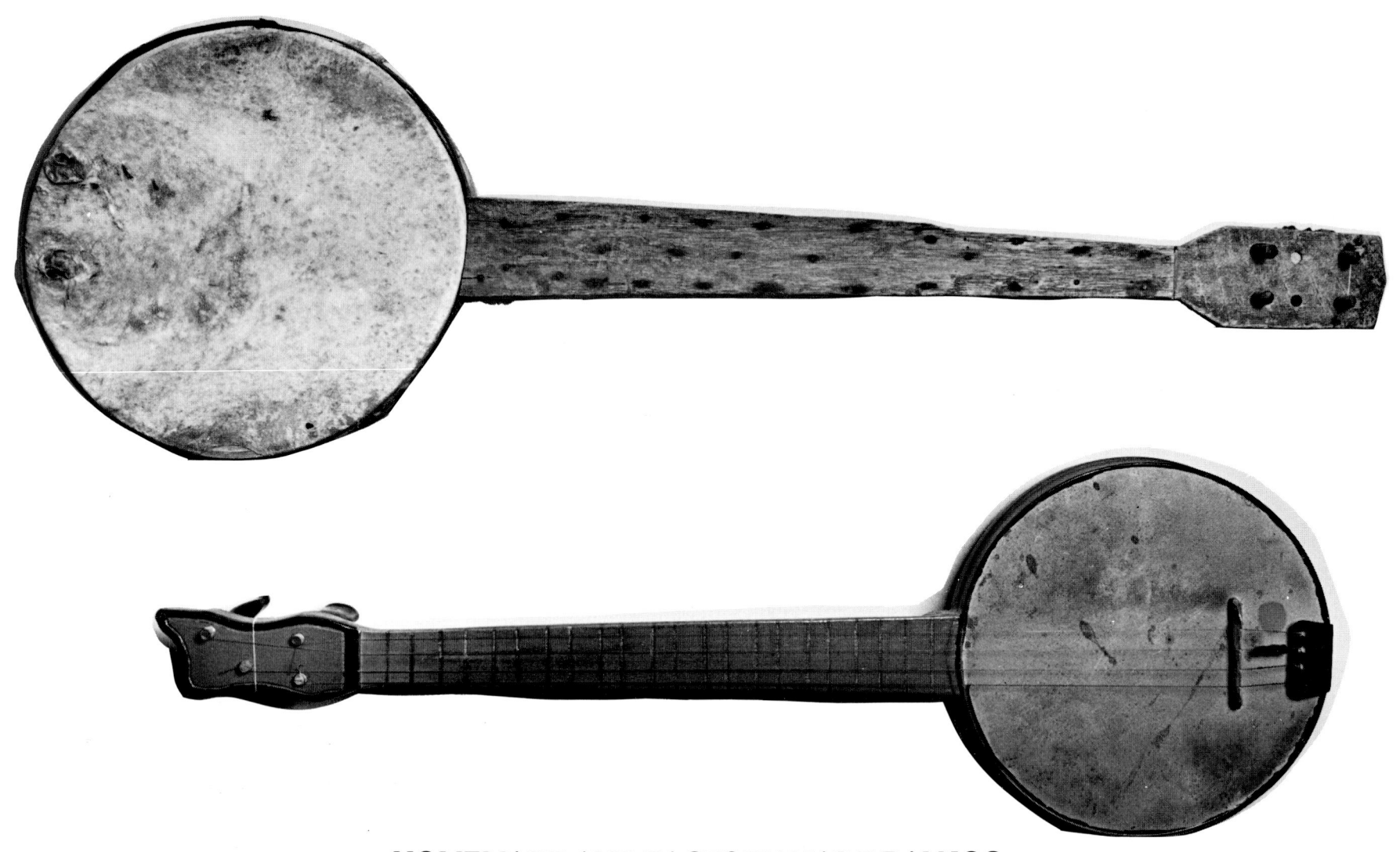

HOMEMADE AND FACTORY MADE BANJOS

The banjo at top, according to Paul Ryan from whom it was purchased, was made in the late 1800's by Victory Crawford of Blair's Gap, near Jonesboro, Tennessee. The neck has evidently been converted from a guitar neck, and the head is of groundhog hide. Note that the ears of the groundhog are still visible on the lower portion of the head. The banjo at the bottom is commercially made and has the brass eagle emblems on the brackets (not shown in the photo). It also was purchased from Paul Ryan of Fall Branch, Tennessee. (Photo by Dana Thomas)

HOMEMADE AND FACTORY MADE BANJOS

Banjos A and C were made by Hiram Sharp who lived in the Cumberland Mountain Community of Cordell near Norma in Scott County, Tennessee. All items except the strings were made of pieces of scrap metal or wood -- nothing was store-bought. The head of C is heavy metal and appears to have been an early outside country store sign. (Sharp also made fiddles and two mouth bows for his own use. They are pictured in their respective categories elsewhere in this booklet, and Sharp is discussed more fully on page 28.)

The banjo pictured in photos B and D was an early factory made one, featuring the American eagle in brass adorning the brackets. It was acquired from Paul Ryan of Falls Branch, near Jonesboro, Tennessee. (Photos by Alan Halbert)

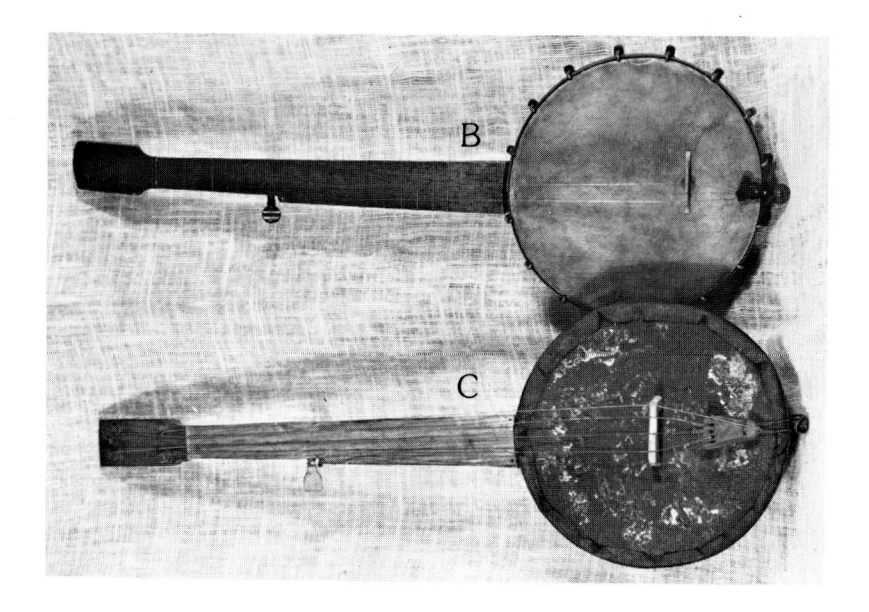

THE HEART BANJO

The heart-shaped design has been used at least since Egyptian times to connote a variety of different, yet similar, sentiments. For the Egyptians it represented the center of intelligence; for the Teutons and Latins, it meant the core or center; for some it had a religious meaning; but for a long time it has symbolized love and friendship. While I have seen it used as the decorative sound holes for some recently made dulcimers, I have seen it only on one other banjo, the Eledge banjo shown in the following photograph.

This completely handmade fretless banjo is made of poplar and put together with square-headed nails. It was acquired by the writer from Professor Roddy Moore of Ferrum, Virginia, but came originally from Hamblen County, Tennessee, near the Great Smoky Mountains. (Photo by Dana Thomas)

KELLIE ELEDGE BANJO

Rufus Eledge and his wife Kellie lived in a pioneer-type log house on Obie's Branch near Bearwaller Mountain on a tiny dirt road at the foot of the Great Smoky Mountains. When I found this old banjo in the attic of the old log loom house in 1964, Kellie said, "Law, that ole banjar has been a'layen around here fer as long as I can recollect".

This homestead was built by old Billy Williams shortly after the American Revolution, and it was there that he reared thirteen of his fifteen children to adulthood. Kellie was a granddaughter.

The banjo was made from an old shoe shipping crate, and the rim is of old signs and tobacco tins. Note the heart-shaped sound hole. (Photo by Wallace Denny)

Rufus Eledge and his fox hounds. (Photo taken in 1964 by the author)

SHERMAN CAMPBELL BANJO

The body of the banjo is made from the metal lid of an oblong cooking pot with a metal "head" applied and painted with yellow strips or decoration. (The back of this banjo still has the handle of the lid attached.) It was purchased about 1968 from the late Sherman Campbell of near the village of Washburn in Grainger County, Tennessee, who I believe made the instrument. The guitar neck has been cut down and converted into one suitable for a banjo. It is now on temporary loan to the Country Music Hall of Fame in Nashville. (Photo by Dana Thomas)

The late Sherman Campbell, who lived in the nearby community of Washburn, Tennessee, made the "cooking lid banjo" shown above. (Photo by the author)

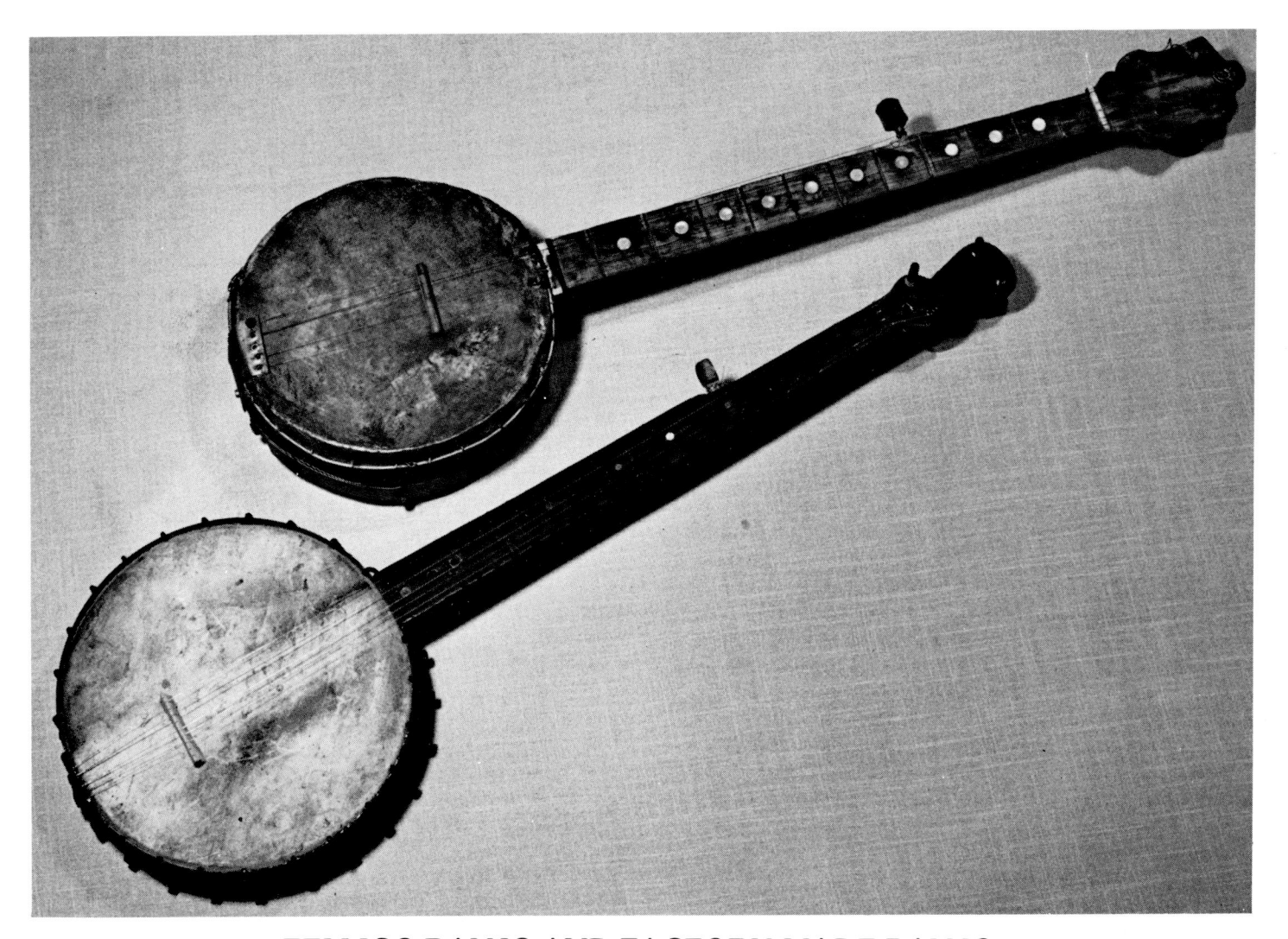

TELLICO BANJO AND FACTORY-MADE BANJO

The banjo shown in the top of the photo was purchased for me by Pat Wink of Clinton at public auction at the famous Tellico mansion in Tellico Plains in southwestern Tennessee in 1976. The mansion was built in 1846 by Elisha Johnson who established a notable iron works there which became of great importance during the Civil War. (General Grant, according to local tradition, once spent the night there.) Although this banjo is crudely made and has the traditional groundhog hide head, it has been "fancied up" in recent years.

The five-string banjo at the bottom is a common factory-made type. The head appears to be seal skin which was applied in the factory. The modern banjos have plastic heads. (Photo by Pat and Bill Miller)

TATE ELLIOTT BANJO

Using a wooden box for the body and a piece of tin for the head, Tate Elliott, as a lad in the early 1900's, made himself a five-string banjo. He then added a little red paint, and he was ready to "make music". Tate still lives (1979) in the Glen Alpine Community, some three miles south of the Museum. (Photo by Pat and Bill Miller)

BURCHETT MULLINS BANJO

Using the frame of a wooden meal sifter as the rim, and a guitar neck, Burchett Mullins, who lived in a remote section of Hancock County known as Blackwater Creek, made "his self a banjar". Several years later he traded it to his neighbor, Noah Bell, a farmer-trader and an all-around mountain man. It was from my friend Noah that I bought the banjo about 1964. Burchett was the son of old Howard Mullins of the same locale, who died at the age of 110. (Photo by Wallace Denny)

LARD CAN BANJO

At the foot of Sutton Ridge on Powell River in Claiborne County, Tennessee, there stood one of the most remote log houses I have seen -- it cannot be reached by automobile even today. This old banjo, believed to have been made by Bob Sutton, came from this quaint place. The neck is made of rough sawn oak, and the body is made of the end of a large tin container called a lard can because of its widespread use in this area to store hog grease or lard when the skins and fat were "rendered" at hog killing time. This container no doubt had developed holes in it and could no longer be used for its intended purpose, hence its conversion into the family musical instrument. (It is presently on loan to the Country Music Hall of Fame in Nashville.) (Photo by Dana Thomas)

Thurman Tinch from Overton County, Tennessee, is shown here in an early photograph (about 1940). Thurman, in addition to being an all-around mountain man, was a banjo picker, 'repairer' and trader. Several of the banjos in the collection were acquired from him. (Photo courtesy of Charles Tinch)

TINCH BANJOS

This fretless banjo at top was bought from my friend, the great horse trader from Monterey, Tennessee -- Ray King. The thin refined walnut neck shows much wear as does the skin head. This banjo was made by his brother-in-law Thurman Tinch using a few factory-made pieces and only six brackets to secure the head.

When the original fingerboard on the banjo at bottom wore too thin, Thurman Tinch, its owner, "half-soled" it by applying a tapering piece of walnut, and by adding new frets. It has a total of thirty-nine brackets, the most I have seen on a banjo. This was the banjo he played in later years. (Photo by Pat and Bill Miller)

BANJO AND WOODEN BANJO CASE

Thurman Tinch also made the walnut neck for this factory-made rim. The head is of groundhog hide and there are 30 brackets to tighten the head. The wooden banjo case, made of poplar wood, is the only one I have seen, which leads me to the conclusion that they were quite rare -- possibly because the instrument was kept at home and was not often carried to parties as were the fiddles. It was acquired from Chris Glen, who acquired it somewhere in western North Carolina. (Photo by Pat and Bill Miller)

UNCLE JIM TINCH BANJO

This banjo belongd to Thurman's father, Uncle Jim Tinch of Overton County, Tennessee. The fretless neck shows much wear. The head, which has been extensively torn, has been sewn back together. (Photo by Wallace Denny)

GOVERNOR TAYLOR'S BANJO?

A letter inside this banjo indicates that it came from the old Hope residence on Kingston Pike in Knoxville. The letter, written by Jack Wayland of Knoxville, states that the Hope daughter married into the Governor Alf Taylor family. According to Guy Bowers, from whom I purchased the instrument, Governor Taylor himself once owned it. It does have the name "Taylor" written in faded script on the bottom side of the head.

Alf Taylor and his brother Bob campaigned against one another for governor of Tennessee in 1896, a political fight which came to be known as the "War of the Roses", after the struggle in England in the late 1400's between members of the royal family. Both eventually served in that office, and Uncle Bob was a Congressman and United States Senator as well.

The eagle-shaped brackets on the instrument are made of brass. The tiny holes in the skin head appear to be shot holes, indicating the groundhog from which the hide came was killed with a shotgun. The head is obviously a replacemnet of the original. (Photo by Pat and Bill Miller)

Retired and disabled with emphysema, Earl Blackwell of Jacksboro in neighboring Campbell County, recalling his boyhood banjo-picking days, decided to make himself one -- or one for the Museum. The neck and peg box are all hand carved, but the head and body are made from an "Old English" fruit cake box. (Photo by Steve Jernigan)

BANJO-GUITAR

The neck and peg box of this instrument are from a guitar, but the body resembles that of a country made banjo. It was acquired from Lee Hill of nearby Tazewell, Tennessee, who bought it there in Claiborne County. This instrument is indicative of the variety and originality of the instruments of this region. (Photo by Steve Jernigan)

THE MOUTH BOW

As a child I remember sitting on the front porch of the home of our next door neighbor, my great uncle Eli Stooksbury, in the late afternoon and listening to him play the mouth bow -- and I thought it was the prettiest music I ever heard. I never knew, or even heard of anyone else who played the mouth bow.

The instrument consisted of a simple bow, not unlike one used as a hunting bow. It was made of red cedar and the "string" was a tiny wire which he unraveled from a piece of door screen. He played it by placing one end of the bow against a firm lower lip and by plucking the string with a rigid finger. The rhythm was acquired by the plucking, and the variation or the pitch was obtained by increasing or decreasing the mouth cavity in much the same manner as when playing the Jews Harp. It was a quarter of a century later that I really became curious about this simple "music bow", its origin, whether mountain people other than Uncle Eli knew the instrument, etc.

My inquiries proved to be productive. My friend, W.G. Lenoir, a man who has collected early artifacts of this area for most of his eighty-eight years, recalled having seen such an instrument just a few miles from the Museum. It belonged to Lawrence Warwick, who lived across the mountain from Andersonville in Dark Hollow. I visited Lawrence several times at his modest home and always thoroughly enjoyed his playing. He used a coin, a twenty-five cent piece, I believe, with the serrated edge to stroke the string. The original bow he played, and which I acquired from him, was also made of cedar.

Lawrence indicated that he learned to play from his father, but he did not know any other family in his community who played the "music bow." Once when I took some television people to his home to film and record his playing, he laughed heartily when we told him of our purpose. "I'm a'feered you've come to a goat's house to get wool", he modestly declared.

In Hancock County, Alex Stewart, the greatest old-time mountain man I have ever known, and my best authority on mountain lore, was very familiar with the mouth bow. And when his interest was revived, he started making them again.

When asked about the origin of the mouth bow, Alex had a ready and plausible answer, as he did for almost any question. "Why, they learned it from the Indians", he said. "The Indians used to live around on Newman's Ridge in my Grandpa's time and they'd set around their campfires of a night and they'd play their hunting bows and the White's sort of took it up from them."

Another Hancock Countian, and also a long time friend, who was familiar with the mouth bow was Tyler Bunch of Snake Hollow. And although he had not "seed one fer years and years" he had not forgotten how it was played as evidenced by the mournful tune which flowed from it when he put it to his lips.

In 1976 I found and purchased two old mouth bows in a most remote section of Scott County, Tennessee, near the community of Norma not far from Senator Howard Baker's home. They were made by Hiram Sharp of hickory and were strung with heavy wire. Along with the two bows, I acquired a banjo and fiddle which had also been made and played by Sharp. These are the only mouth bows I have seen or heard of which are more than forty or fifty years old.

It has been said that the mouth bow is the father, or is it the mother, of all stringed instruments. Ripley's "Believe It Or Not" recently pictured a native woman from the New Britain Islands playing an instrument almost identical to the mountain mouth bow. It was called a pangola, and was apparently a part of a most primitive culture.

It appears that the use of the mouth bow in Appalachia, like the dulcimer, was known throughout the region. But like the dulcimer, it was known by relatively few in any given area. I have found more people in Hancock County, Tennessee, than elsewhere who were familiar with the mouth bow -- also called the music bow and the tuning bow.

The great Alex Stewart, at the age of 86, plays the mouth bow he made at his home on Panther Creek in Hancock County, Tennessee. Alex was reared in a small log house on Newman's Ridge, home of the Melungeons, a still unexplained group of people who were living there when the first White settlers arrived in the 1700's. Alex says that his grandfather told him that the Whites learned to play the mouth bow from the Indians who played their hunting bows in the evenings as they sat around their camps. (Photo by the author)

Uncle Eli Stooksbury was our closest neighbor on the Mountain Road in Anderson County, Tennessee, and the first person I ever heard who played the mouth bow. (Photo courtesy of Carlock Stooksbury)

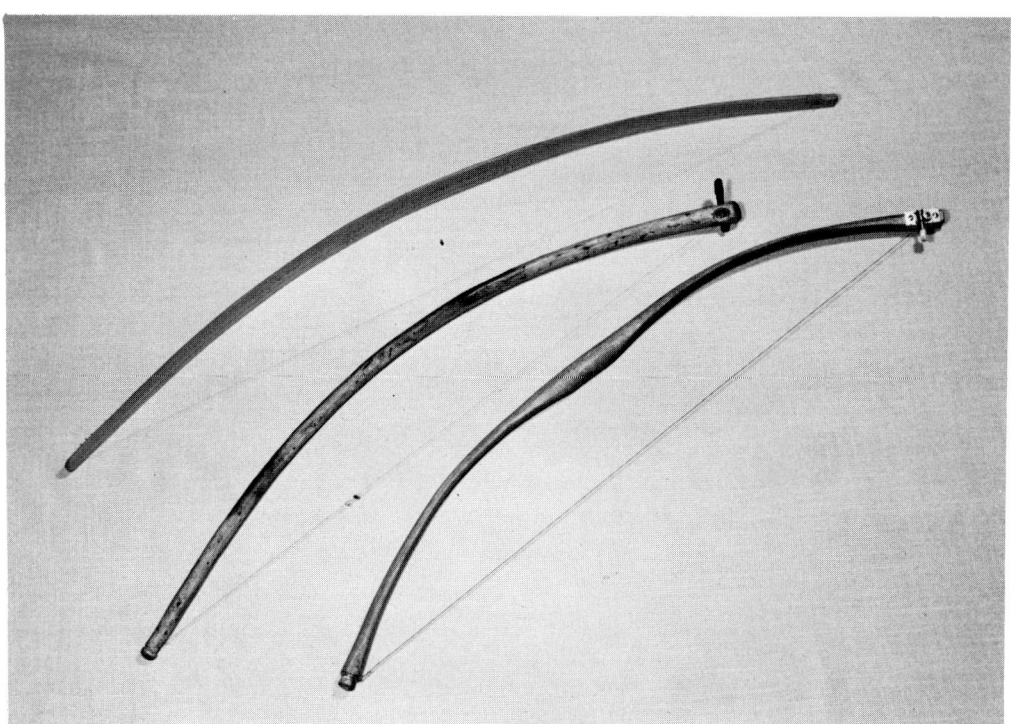

MOUTH BOWS

The red cedar mouth bow, top left, was made for me in 1968 by my old friend, Alex Stewart of Panther Creek in Hancock County. It is similar to the one owned by his grandfather, Boyd Stewart of Newman's Ridge, also from Hancock County.

The center mouth bow was made and played by Lawrence Warwick who lived in Dark Hollow, some five miles east of the Museum. He used the wooden tuning peg to increase and decrease tension on the single string.

The bow at right was made by my friend and neighbor, the late Chuck Lambdin of Glen Alpine. While Alex Stewart made his bows of cedar, Chuck made this one of hickory. Alex had three tiny tacks to increase the tension on the bow, but Chuck used a single key from an old guitar to accomplish the same purpose. (Photo by Pat and Bill Miller)

Tyler Bunch, right, my old friend from Snake Hollow in Hancock County, explains to me how he learned to play the mouth bow three-quarters of a century ago. He is shown here on the porch of his house, holding a cedar mouth bow -- one made by Alex Stewart. (Photo by Wallace Denny)

The late Lawrence Warwick of Dark Hollow, some six miles east of the Museum, is the only old timer I have known who used a coin (a twenty-five cent piece) to strike the bow string. "I learnt to play the music bow from my Pap," he said. (Photo by the author)

HIRAM SHARP MOUTH BOW

This is one of two or three old mouth bows I have found in the mountains. It was made and played by Hiram Sharp (1885-1976) who was born and lived all his life at the old Hurricane place at Cordell, four miles from Norma in Scott County, Tennessee. He was a sawmill man and logger for the big New River Lumber Company of Norma. He also repaired guns, clocks, etc. In addition to the mouth bow, Hiram made and played the fiddle and banjo. (Photo by Alan Halbert)

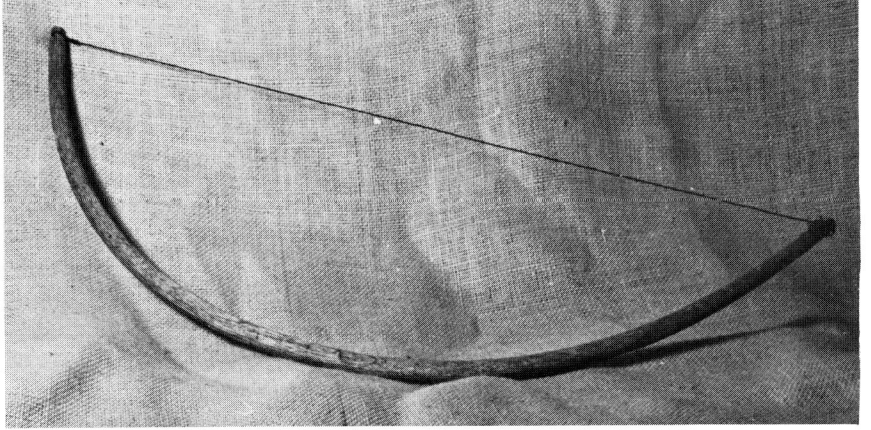

THE APPALACHIAN DULCIMER

How many times have I read "authoritarian" statements indicating that the "dulcimer was the traditional instrument of the folk of Southern Appalachia"? Some would have us believe that there was a dulcimer hanging inside every cabin. My experience indicates that this is simply not true.

Fully eighty to ninety percent of the older persons in Appalachia, with whom I have talked, had never even heard of the dulcimer until recent years. It is true that it was made and played by some of the old mountain people, who pronounced it "dulcymore" or "delcymore", but its existence was spotty, to say the least. In fact, I doubt that its usage prior to the 1940's was as commonplace as the mouth bow.

Professor J. Allen Smith has traveled throughout the Eastern part of the country for years, ferreting out every dulcimer he heard of, and conducting exhaustive research on the subject. His extensive book on the dulcimer is now being published. He stated several years ago that the Museum of Appalachia contained the largest collection he had found in the country. And at that time the number of our dulcimers was substantially smaller than at present.

Charles K. Wolfe, in his well-researched book on the development of country music in Tennessee, **Tennessee Strings,** does not even list the dulcimer in his index. Ralph Lee Smith, the dulcimer researcher from Washington, D.C. (no relation to Professor Allen Smith mentioned earlier), estimates that there were probably no more than 1,000 dulcimers in all of the Appalachian region prior to the recent revival of the instrument. These facts are indicative, I think, of the scarcity of this instrument.

The word "dulcimer" is believed to have been taken from the "hammered dulcimer" which was used in England and which dates back to Biblical times. (The word "dulce" in Greek means "sweet", and "melos" in Latin means "song".)

The origin of the mountain, or plucked dulcimer, and its scattered, yet rather widespread usage in the Appalachian Mountains, is still somewhat of a mystery. Its origin seems to have been in northern Europe, the German "scheitholt" being one of its oldest ancestors. The scheitholt was mentioned in German writings as early as 1618, and like its descendant, the mountain dulcimer, it was both plucked and played with a bow. According to Michael Murphy in **The Appalachian Dulcimer Book,** the scheitholt was adopted in Sweden, Norway, Iceland, France and Holland. In each of these countries the shape and style of the instrument took on local characteristics.

The scheitholt-type instrument was found in Pennsylvania, at least as early as the 1770's and perhaps earlier. This instrument was long, narrow and straight-sided, and the fingerboard was made onto the body of the instrument. The scheitholt instruments in the famous Mercer Museum in Pennsylvania are very similar to those of early German origin. But as the dulcimer was developed in southern Appalachia, the fingerboard was almost always raised, and the instrument took on a variety of curvacious shapes. They were seldom straight-sided and rectangular, as they seemed to have been in the Pennsylvania area. And they became more crude, less refined, and more diversified in style, decoration, and construction. Why the mountaineer changed the German-type instrument into its present shape and form is still being studied by students of the subject.

Although its roots go back a long way, the mountain dulcimer, as we know it, is of relatively recent origin, not even as old as the banjo. Ralph Lee Smith, mentioned above, has spent much time researching the subject and he feels that most of these instruments were made between 1875 and 1910. Neither he nor I ever heard a claim that the dulcimer was made prior to the Civil War.

The mountain dulcimer, rare in Appalachia, was of course much more so in other regions; hence, it is interesting that "Harper's Magazine" carried a story in 1909 titled "The Dulcimer." In it the young blacksmith in an unnamed mountain region made the instrument for his lover. He had gotten the pattern from a remote mountain region.

Although I have not found enough of these instruments to indicate a definitive pattern, there are some areas where they appear to be more common than in other areas. In Lee County and Scott County, in Virginia, and in Hancock County, Tennessee, I have encountered more than in any other area with which I am familiar. In Anderson County where the Museum is located, I have not found or even heard of a single one.

The mountain dulcimer was, in my opinion, almost extinct when some mountain singers revived it at the last moments. In 1925, for example, a noted researcher, Josiah H. Combs, stated, "The dulcimer is an instrument formerly used but falling rapidly into decay." Among the most acclaimed of those responsible for reviving the dulcimer was Jean Ritchie, the youngest girl of twelve children, from near the eastern Kentucky village of Viper.

When Jean went to New York she took her dulcimer with her, was "discovered", and soon became known throughout the country. She is perhaps the best-known traditional folk singer today. And with her phenomenal success also came phenomenal interest in this "new" instrument called the dulcimer. Dulcimer makers sprang up everywhere -- but these instruments were new and glossy, and constructed with glue and often had the "factory-made" look. The crude construction, awkward attempts at decoration, improvised frets, etc. of the old type mountain dulcimers were largely gone. But it is good that the tradition lives on, and that the instrument has gained such widespread notoriety.

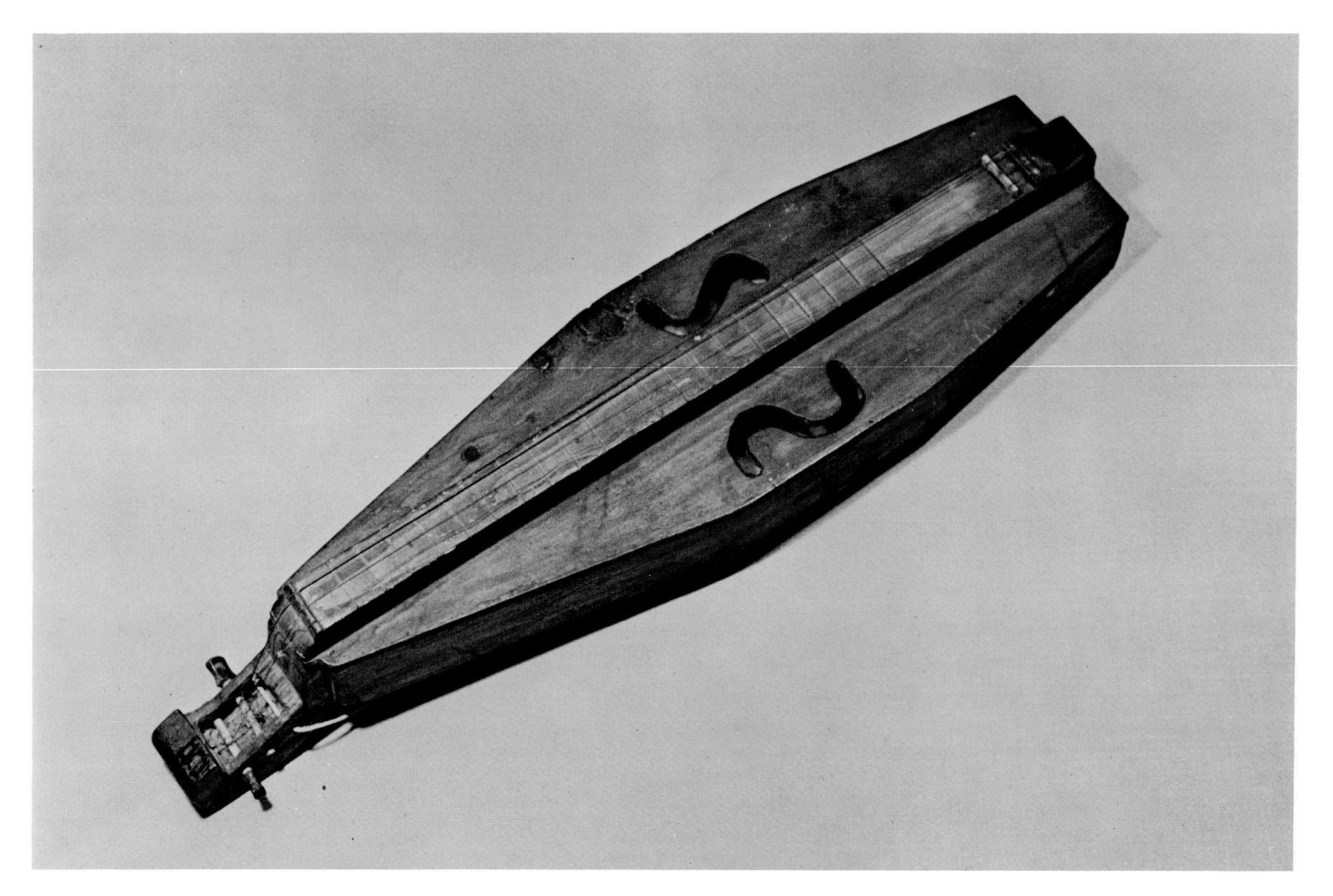

PUTNAM COUNTY DULCIMER
This most crude dulcimer was purchased from Ray King of Monterey. He bought it somewhere in the mountains of Putnam County, Tennessee, but didn't know its precise origin. It resembles other instruments I have seen in the Cumberland Mountains of Middle Tennessee. (Photo by Pat and Bill Miller)

MRS. JOHN CARRICO WITH HER DULCIMER

Mrs. Carrico, of near Fort Blackmore in Scott County, Virginia, holds the old family dulcimer. It is the only one I have seen which has no fingerboard whatever. Her late husband, John Carrico, once told me that it was noted by using a pocket knife, in much the same manner that the dobro and steel guitar are noted. (Photo by the author)

CAMPBELL COUNTY DULCIMER

This pine dulcimer originated in the little mountain community of White Oak in neighboring Campbell County, Tennessee. White Oak is located in the Cumberland Mountains in a coal producing region some fifteen miles southeast of Jellico, Tennessee, and a few miles south of Bell County, Kentucky. This instrument, which has a total of 26 frets, was purchased from Reba Morton of Jacksboro, Tennessee. (Photo by Pat and Bill Miller)

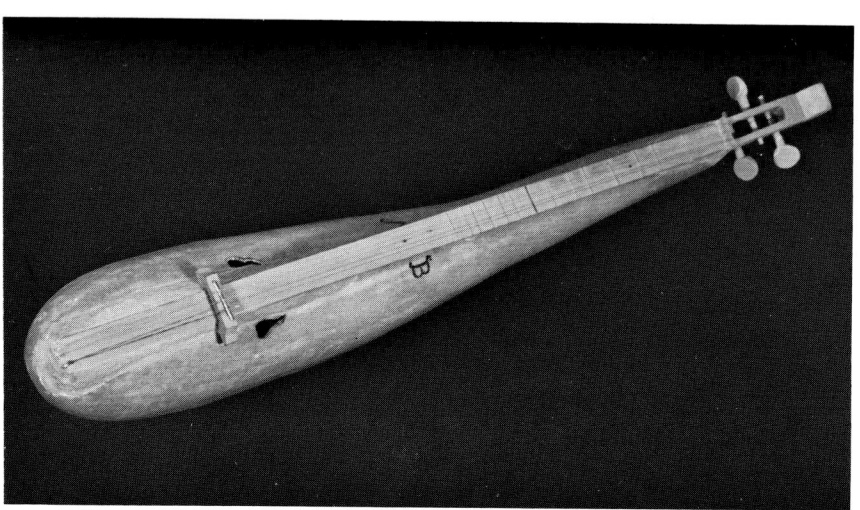

GOURD DULCIMERS

These gourds were planted, nurtured, raised, and then made into dulcimers by Minnie Black of East Bernstadt (near London), Kentucky. In addition to making dulcimers and fiddles from gourds, Minnie makes them into snakes, fowl, people, and animals of all sorts. She lives alone, makes the entire instrument herself, including the fingerboard, tuning pegs, etc. (There is a collection of over 200 gourd 'creatures' in a separate exhibit in the Museum.) (Photo by Pat and Bill Miller)

HAMMERED DULCIMERS

It has been said that the hammered dulcimer was the forerunner of the piano. The basic similarity is that both instruments have numerous strings (54 and 48 respectively on these two) and that the sound is produced by striking the strings. In the case of the dulcimer the strings are struck with slender wooden sticks held in one's hand, whereas the piano is more mechanized.

The instrument at the top, apparently factory made, was purchased from John Maxwell, the well-known craftsman and dulcimer maker of Cookeville, Tennessee. It is constructed of pine and has what appears to be mahogany veneer on the edge and on a portion of the front.

The bottom instrument was purchased from Robert Weems of Knoxville and is presently on loan to the Country Music Hall of Fame in Nashville. (Photo by Dana Thomas)

THE DORA MULLINS BOWED DULCIMER

This dulcimer, the only one I have ever seen with an accompanying bow, was purchased from Earl Mullins (shown above) of Lee County, Virginia. It had belonged to his mother, Dora Mullins, and prior to that to her mother.

Earl recalls seeing his mother play the dulcimer on a table (the dulcimer has tiny "feet" on its base) when using the bow. But when using a quill, as in the usual fashion of playing the dulcimer, she would hold it in her lap. The bow is hand-made and quite crude and is strung with hair from a mule's tail.

The early Mullins homeplace was located in a small community called McClure's Chapel in Lee County, Virginia, near the Powel River and the Hancock County, Tennessee, line. When asked if there were other dulcimers in that area, Earl recalled hearing of only one other. It had belonged to "old Aunt Vestie Houndshell", a sister to his grandmother.

Earl seems to recall having heard that his dulcimer was made by an old man named Willie Speaks who had lived near there on Powell River. The design is quite similar to some others from that general area. (Photo by the author)

THE BILL AND DORA MULLINS FAMILY

Dora Mullins, shown here sitting beside her husband Bill Mullins, and with seven of her children, learned to play the dulcimer from her mother. Their home was in a remote section of Lee County, Virginia, near Powell River and not far from the Tennessee line. Earl, from whom I purchased the bowed dulcimer, is shown at left on the back row. (Photo courtesy of Bill Mullins)

COCKE COUNTY DULCIMER

This dulcimer is characteristic of the upper East Tennessee-North Carolina type, and was purchased from an old Cocke County, Tennessee, estate at public auction by Hazel Godwin of Morristown. It was from Mrs. Godwin that I purchased it in 1973. (Photo by Pat and Bill Miller)

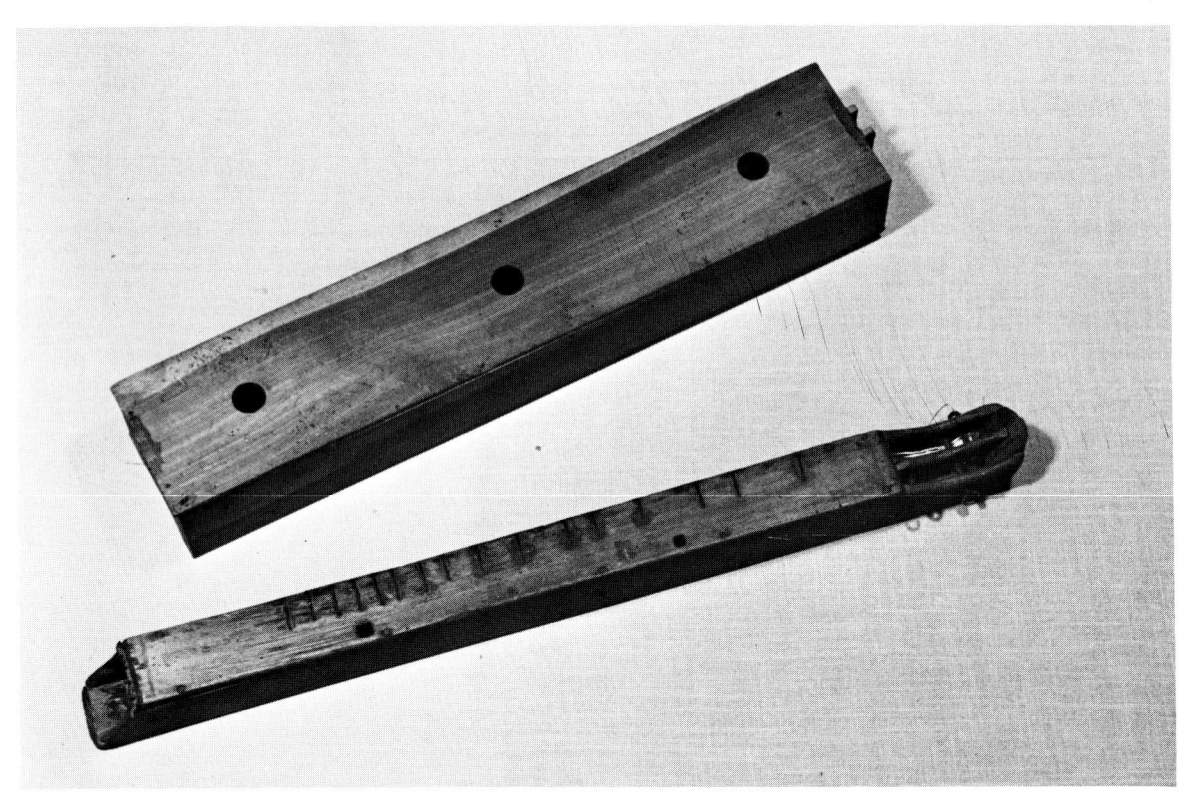

DULCIMER OR SCANTLING
(top photo)

When I was a young boy I recall hearing my Grandfather Irwin refer to a long rectangular plank as a scantling. I never heard that term used again until Allen Smith, who had studied the American dulcimer more than anyone I know, called the instrument pictured above a "scantling". It has many characteristics of a dulcimer -- but it also perfectly rectangular, similar in its simple style to the plank my grandfather called a scantling. I wonder if there is a connection. One of the old meanings of the word is a piece of timber less than eight inches wide and from two to eight inches in thickness.

This instrument is made of cedar and was purchased from Roddy Moore of Ferrum College in Virginia. I believe its origin was middle Tennessee.

EARLY APPALACHIAN DULCIMER OR SCHEITHOLT (bottom photo)

Of all the instruments in the collection, none has been of more interest to the students of early American instruments than the one shown in the bottom section of this photograph. I purchased it from Roddy Moore of Ferrum College who bought it from Ruby Warren who had a small shop in Candler, North Carolina. She informed me that it came from the mountains of North Carolina near Asheville. It is made entirely of pine, put together with square cut nails, and has the old type cotter keys for pegs. It was once painted green with what appears to be buttermilk paint. The fingerboard shows much wear -- more than any other dulcimer in the display.

It is very similar to the German scheitholts made in the 1700's, the instrument from which the Appalachian dulcimer sprang. (Photo by Pat and Bill Miller)

GEORGE JOHNSON DULCIMER

George Allen Johnson is shown here at his home on Blackwater Creek on the Virginia-Tennessee line with the dulcimer he made about 1930. When asked what prompted him to make the instrument, he replied, "Well, I recollect hearing old Hugh Brooks playin' an old 'dulcymore' when I's jest a boy. He lived way over yonder on Clinch River, down below Kyles Ford."

I asked George if the women ever played it, if there were other dulcimers in the area, and how old the Brooks instrument was.

"Lord, son, I couldn't tell you who made it - hit was an old relic the first time ever I seed it (about 1915). Don't recollect anybody playing it except the old man Brooks. And Lord, he could make it talk. He wuz the one who learnt me to play - and hit was the only dulcymore that I ever seed 'til here of late - and now you hear tell of em all the time." (Photos by the author)

DULCIMER, OR HUMLE

Sallie Swor, a full-time employee of the Museum of Appalachia, is shown here with the humle, one of the most mysterious and interesting instruments I have found. It is very similar to the humle which was developed in Holland, Sweden and perhaps in other Scandanavian countries. (Humle is a derivation of the Dutch verb hommeln, meaning to hum.) Like the Appalachian dulcimer, the humle descended from the German scheitholt.

The iron turning pegs are like those of the Swedish instrument as are the several drone strings not noted. One side is straight while the other has a pronounced bulge. These and other features suggest that it is of direct European influences, if not of European construction. But the crude wire frets, the type construction, etc. seem to indicate that it was made in Appalachia.

I purchased the instrument from Mary Ellen Walker of Morristown, Tennessee, who bought it from a small "junk" shop in the same town. The owner of the shop bought it at an auction at nearby Bean Station where many local items were sold, but which also included "some Ohio stuff". (Photo by the author)

NORTH CAROLINA DULCIMER

This pine dulcimer originated in the mountains near Asheville, North Carolina. It was found by Professor Roddy Moore of Ferrum College, in Ferrum, Virginia, from whom I purchased it. It is unusual in that it has no frets, nor does it appear to ever have had any. The small nail holes may have been made to indicate the intervals of the frets for noting purposes. (Photo by Pat and Bill Miller)

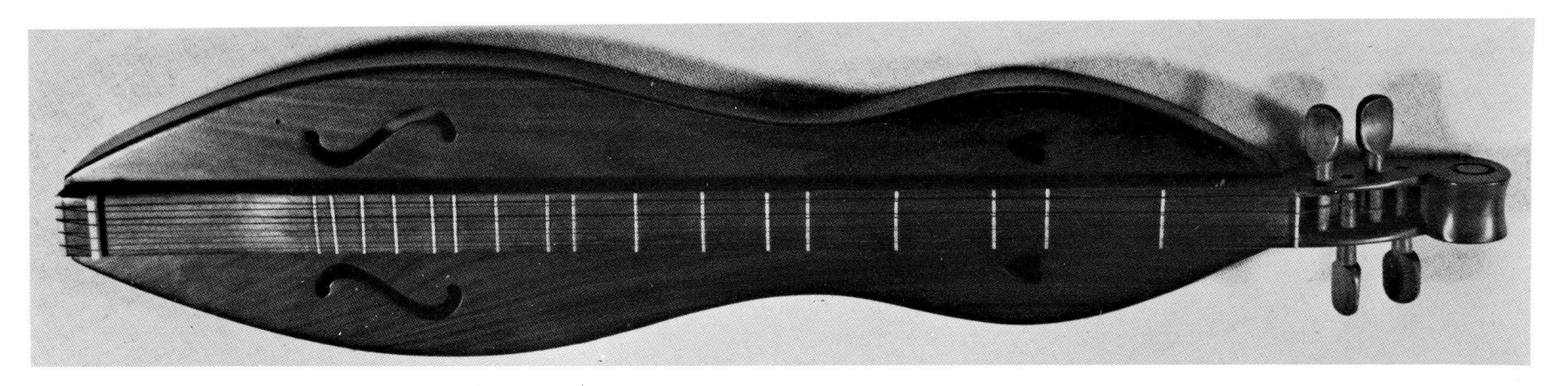

DON WARD DULCIMER

The only new instrument in the collection, this dulcimer, was made by one of Tennessee's most noted craftsmen, Don Ward, about 1960, then of Pleasant Hill in Cumberland County, Tennessee. It is reputed to have been the first one he made. Note that his instrument has the hourglass shape, while none of the early dulcimers in the collection are so designed. This shaped dulcimer seems rather characteristic of the Kentucky instruments. (Photo by Pat and Bill Miller)

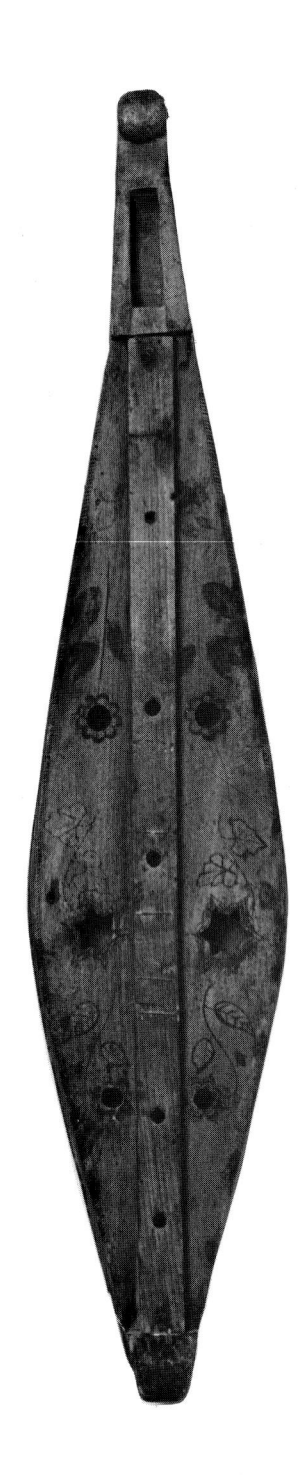

THAD BAYS DULCIMER

This most interesting dulcimer was found underneath a pile of rubbish in a falling-down old smoke house at the Ely place in Lee County, Virginia, near Rose Hill and the Tennessee line. I had searched the building once and was ready to leave when I happened to remove some old sacks and papers which revealed a tiny portion of the instrument. Ely, from whom I purchased it and who was born about 1896, said it had been there for as long as he could recall, but he knew nothing more of its history.

It is the only dulcimer I have found with an inscribed name on it -- that of "Thad Bays." Since the signature appears to have the same coloration and style as the floral design, I assume that Bays was the maker of the instrument, and not necessarily the owner.

The floral decorations, in which the sound holes serve as the center of the flower, are remarkably similar to the design on the Maw Barnett dulcimer from the Virginia-Tennessee line near Gate City, Virginia. The number of petals, for example, is the same on the flowers on both instruments. It is about forty miles over mountainous terrain between the two points where the dulcimers were found. One can only surmise that they were either made by the same person, or that one instrument was the inspiration for the other. The instruments are presently on loan to the Country Music Hall of Fame in Nashville. (Photo by Dana Thomas)

Jean Schilling, one of the country's best known dulcimer players and singers of traditional mountain songs, is shown here playing a dulcimer she and her husband Lee made. Jean has just completed a book, **"Old Time Fiddle Tunes for the Appalachian Dulcimer"**. The Schillings reside in the small East Tennessee town of Cosby.

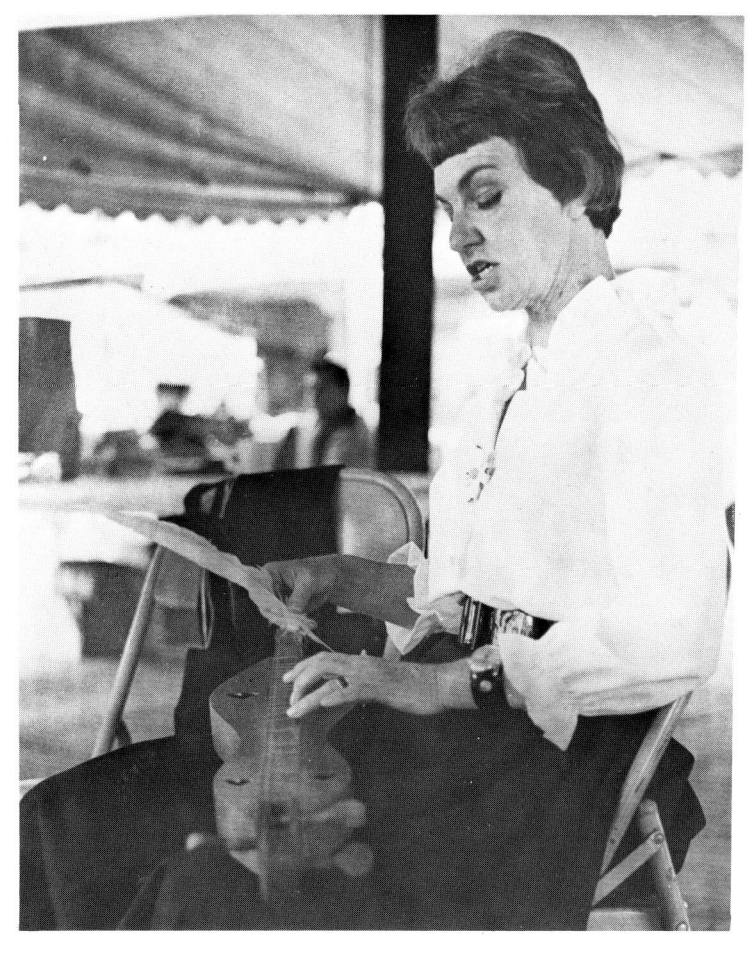

Alberta Prulock Brewer of Norris is shown using the traditional goose feather to strum the dulcimer as she sings. Alberta, a native of southern Georgia, was enchanted with the Appalachian dulcimer when she was exposed to it upon coming to live in East Tennessee. She was especially impressed after talking with Ed Presnell, the well-known dulcimer maker from Banner Elk, North Carolina. After her husband, Carson, purchased one for her as a gift from Presnell, she learned quickly, and was soon playing for her own entertainment and for illustrative purposes in her talks on the dulcimer before the various clubs and gatherings in this area. Through her influence, many others have "taken up" the instrument.

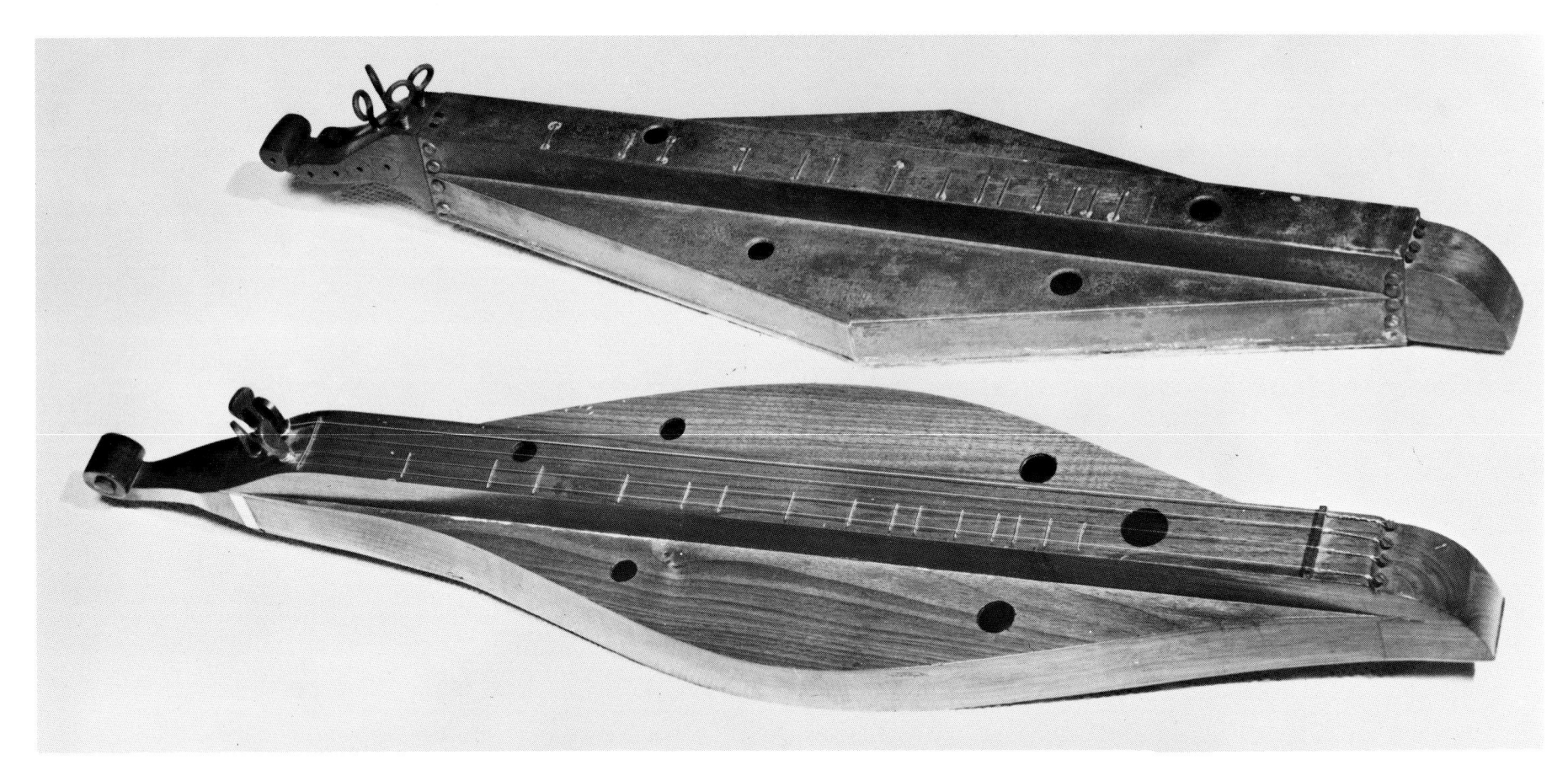

THE POWELL CROSBY DULCIMERS

These two interesting dulcimers came from the old Crosby mansion, located on Holston River, a few miles north of Morristown, Tennessee. They belonged to the late Powell H. Crosby, last occupant of this old homestead prior to its removal preparatory to the construction of Cherokee Dam.

The top instrument is especially interesting as the entire body is made of tin. It is believed to have been made by Andrew J. Robertson (1867-1955), a lifelong tinsmith of Morristown. Shirley Crosby Hodges recalls, as a child, her father taking this dulcimer from its "case", an old white cotton sack, and playing it in the evenings for the family. She later acquired it, along with the wooden dulcimer, from the family estate.

According to research conducted by Mrs. Hodges, the wooden dulcimer, shown in the bottom portion of the picture, was made in Morristown by one James T. Holley. He was the son of W.T. Holley who had a cabinetmaker's shop there in the late 1800's; but the instruments were believed to have been made in the early part of this century. (Photograph courtesy of Shirley Crosby Hodges)

Shown here is an artist's drawing (from an old photograph) of the Crosby homeplace from whence the two dulcimers, shown on the opposite page, came; evidence that not all dulcimers came from the one room cabin. The photo of the three instruments, shown at left, was taken about 1940 on the front porch of the old Crosby home. (Photo and drawing courtesy of Shirley Crosby Hodges)

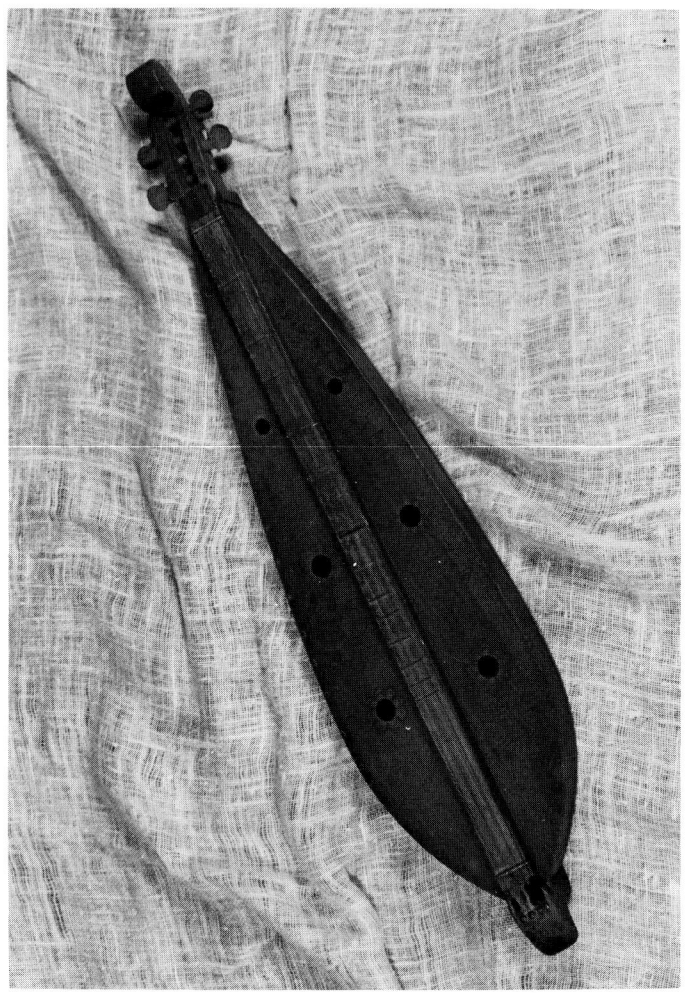

MAW BARNETT DULCIMER

    This decorated dulcimer was my first old one -- acquired from Guy Bowers then of Kingsport, Tennessee, about 1963. It had belonged, he said, to old Maw Barnett of Lynn Gardens, a community located between Kingsport and Scott County, Virginia, on Daniel Boone's famous wilderness road.
    This instrument is very similar to others from southwest Virginia (Lee and Scott Counties). The scroll of the neck, the sound holes, the floral designs, and the general shape are remarkably similar. Note that the sound holes serve as the center of the flower. (Photo by Alan Halbert)

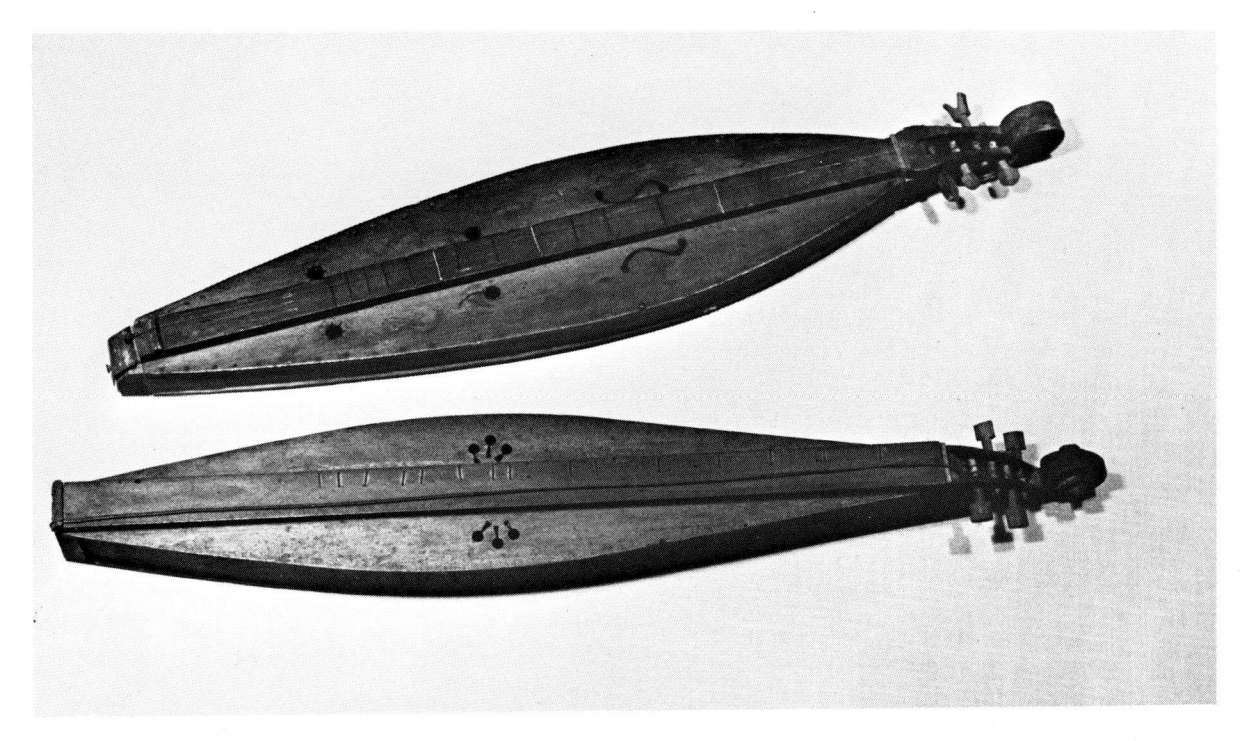

SAM WHITE DULCIMER AND JOHN McLAIN DULCIMER
(Both made in the same area of upper East Tennessee)

The dulcimer at the top was made in the late 1880's by Sam White at his ancestral home near Lost Mountain in the Baileytown community of Greene County, Tennessee. After he died several years ago the instrument remained in the old homeplace with his unmarried sister, Bonnie White. She sold it to Paul Ryan and I bought it from him on Christmas Day, 1975.

Sam had worked in the coal mines of southwestern Virginia (Wise and Lee Counties, I believe) and 'got the idea' of making a dulcimer after seeing and hearing one in that area. It is very similar to three other dulcimers I have acquired in that locale. It, like the others, has intricate, but faded, art work over much of the exterior and is similar in design. According to his sister, Sam White had never seen a dulcimer in his own community, but "borrowed" the idea from the southwestern Virginia section.

The shape and design of the bottom dulcimer is similar to the one made by White and to those I have found in upper East Tennessee. I purchased it from David Byrd of Erwin, Tennessee, who bought it, along with an old handmade fiddle, from the old J.S. McLain homeplace near Baileytown, the same community where White lived, but across the line in Greene County. The "key-hole" sound holes are different from any design I have seen. It originally had twenty-one wire frets. I have heard that John McLain, who died in 1942, was a fiddle maker -- maybe he made this dulcimer also. (Photo by Pat and Bill Miller)

SPEARS FERRY DULCIMER

The unusual, perhaps unique feature, of this dulcimer is that it has the musical scale carved on the raised fingerboard. It was acquired about 1966 from Guy Bowers, who stated that it came from Spears Ferry in Scott County, Virginia, on the Clinch River near the Tennessee line. Spears Ferry was on Daniel Boone's early trail extending from North Carolina into Kentucky.

This instrument once belonged, Guy informed me, to a Dr. Pollard of that community. (Photos by Dana Thomas)

MISCELLANEOUS INSTRUMENTS OF SOUTHERN APPALACHIA
(Guitar, Mandolin, Jews Harp, Harmonica, etc.)

Although the fiddle and the banjo, and to a much lesser extent the dulcimer and mouthbow, were popular early instruments of this region, a variety of other instruments have been used at various times. A very brief consideration is given to these instruments along with photographs of those in the display at the Museum.

One of the dramatic changes in the musical style in this area in the early part of the twentieth century was the formation of the string band - and with this advent came the introduction of the guitar. It had not been a popular instrument with the common people in our region prior to that time.

There are several possible reasons for the rather rapid popularity of the guitar. First, thousands of mountain boys returned home in 1900 from Puerto Rico and Cuba where they had been pleasantly exposed to the instrument during their service in the Spanish-American War. Then the mail order catalog was becoming popular and it advertised the guitar for a few dollars. Probably one of the greatest boosts it ever received in this region was in 1927 when Ralph Peer, working for Victor Recording Company, discovered the Carter family in Bristol, Tennessee.

"Mother" Maybelle Carter, in particular, became exceptionally popular as a guitar player. Her most popular song was "The Wildwood Flower", and it undoubtedly inspired more young boys, at least in the South, to want to play the guitar than any other song ever written.

As a young boy I recall hearing Archie Campbell, then known only as "Grandpappy", play "The Wildwood Flower" on Knoxville's famous noonday program, The Mid-Day Merry-go-round. I thought it was the prettiest tune I ever heard, and my greatest ambition was to learn to play it. When I was twelve I bought an old Stella guitar from my cousin Amos Stooksbury for four dollars. I had no idea how to even tune it and got my Uncle Frank Atkins to take me to Bob Cox's place in the "gap of the mountain" to have it tuned. (Bob was, and is today, a great old-time fiddler who now plays with our group.)

But while the guitar was becoming very popular in the 1930's, it had not been a familiar instrument with many of the old timers. Asa Martin of Estill County, Kentucky, who was a well-known performer in the 1920's and 1930's, told me recently that he clearly remembers the first guitar he ever saw -- and that it was somewhat of a novelty. An 1886 photograph taken at the old market house in Knoxville shows four prominent citizens playing fiddles -- but no guitars or any other instrument was included. (One of the group was Bob Taylor who was later to become Governor of Tennessee.) Similarly, a photograph of the famous Fiddlin' John Carson taken in 1919 shows three other fiddlers and one banjo, but no guitar or mandolin.

Like the guitar, the mandolin was a late-comer to the music scene in southern Appalachia. It is paradoxical, then, that the "Father of Bluegrass", Bill Monroe, was a mandolin player. Today, a bluegrass band is not complete unless it contains a mandolin.

A photograph included in Wolfe's book taken at the Mountain City Fiddler's Convention in 1925 is perhaps illustrative of the relative prominence which the mandolin "played" in East Tennessee music at that time. Although some thirty musicians are shown in the photograph with their instruments, only one of the entire group was shown with a mandolin. A 1929 photograph of the "Grand Ole Opry" shows a group of about forty-five, with fiddles, banjos, and several guitars, but not a single mandolin.

The Jews harp and the harmonica, most often called a French harp in this area, have been a part of the music of this region since the first settlers came in the 1700's. Remnants of these two instruments are often found in the ruins of the earliest military forts in this area.

Jim McCarroll, at left, plays his music box with his friend, Jim Russell, a well-known old-time fiddler from nearby Clinton. "Uncle" Jim of neighboring Roane County, is one of the great old-time fiddlers, having won over sixty contests in the twenties and thirties. He formed a band called "The Roane County Ramblers" and was later recorded by Columbia -- and at least one of the 1929 records has been re-recorded on a modern type record. His "box" consists of a single wire stretched across the center, attached on one end only. The unattached end of the wire is tied to a short stick which he holds in his left hand. And as he plucks the string with his right hand, he increases and decreases the tension on the wire with his left, thereby varying the pitch and playing any tune he pleases. This is the only such instrument I have seen or heard of -- he said he learned to play it from his grandmother, who was part Cherokee from North Carolina. (Photo by the author)

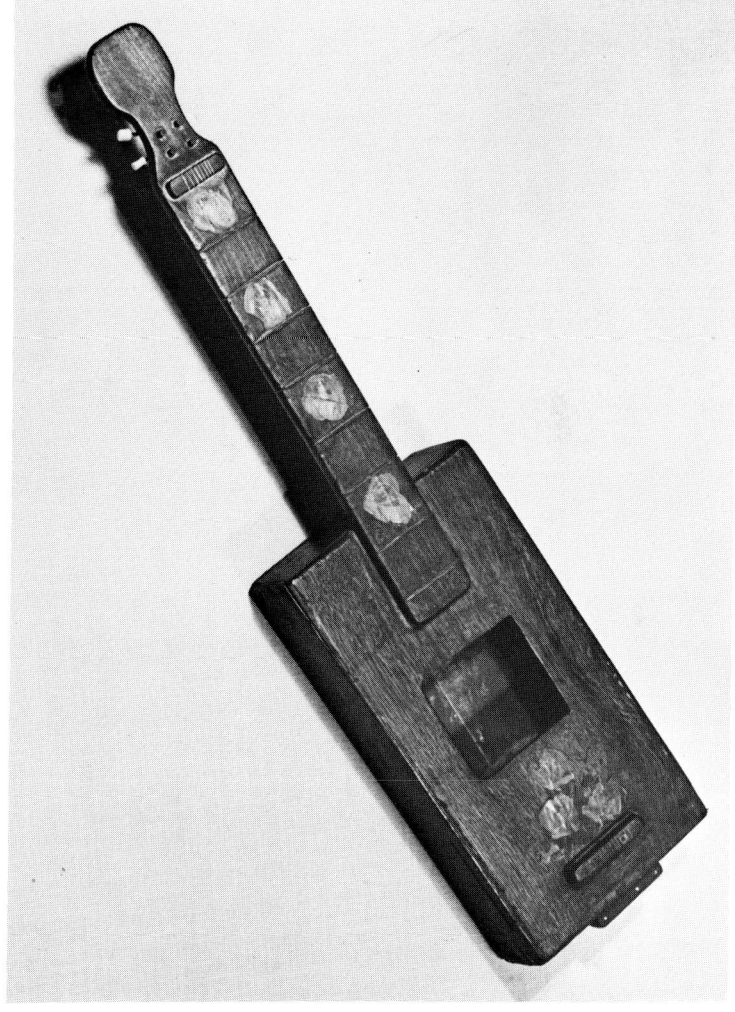

EARLY GUITAR AND PATTERN

This is the earliest factory-made guitar I have found -- dating back, I believe, to near the Civil War period. It belonged to the late Luther Hill of Union County, Tennessee (later of Knoxville) and it was from his daughter, Florence Allred of Sevierville, that I bought it. The crude guitar gig, or form, was used as a pattern for making the body of the guitar, (but not the one shown in the photograph). It was purchased from Lee Hill of nearby Claiborne County. (Photo by Pat and Bill Miller)

GUITAR BANJO?

Here is an instrument which I am unable to categorize as either a banjo or guitar. It has eight grooves in the bridge - indicating eight strings; so perhaps it is a mandolin. It is certainly lavishly decorated, and has been made for some time. It was purchased from a trader who acquired it somewhere in the middle Tennessee area. (Photo by Pat and Bill Miller)

THE MAIL ORDER GUITAR

Although the possessions of the Esco Glandon family, living in this one room log house were few, they were able to afford this new mail order guitar. This photograph was taken in 1933 when the guitar was "catching on" in this region. The Glandon home was located about 15 miles northeast of the Museum at Bridges Chapel near old Loyston. Glandon, who was a tenent farmer, or sharecropper, worked three years in Kokomo, Indiana, returned to his native home, rebuilt the cabin and went back to farming. (Note the numerous floral arrangements, the children's school work displayed prominently, and the fact that there was only one chair.) (Photo by Louis Hines with T.V.A.)

"ELVIS GUITAR"

Influenced by the colorful, rhinestone costumes and instruments of some of the later so-called country music people, a Crossville, Tennessee, man decorated this cheap instrument and called it his "Elvis Presley" guitar. He sold it to Ray King, my trader friend of Monterey, and when Ray was presenting his sales pitch, he said, "Now, I ain't guaranteeing that they's some real diamonds and real pearls amongst all that jewelry, but they might be. A body would think that they'd be at least one real pearl, or one real diamond in all that mess, now wouldn't he?" And with such pleasant possibilities, who could not risk the gamble? (Photo by Pat and Bill Miller)

HOMER HARRIS GUITAR

During the 1930's and 1940's Homer Harris was a household word in East Tennessee because of his daily appearance on the most popular noonday radio program in Knoxville called the "Mid-Day Merry-Go-Round". He was called the "six-foot-six singing cowboy". This instrument was purchased from Lennie Campbell of Clinton who states she bought it from Harris' mother. Homer is still performing for schools throughout the region. (Photo by Pat and Bill Miller)

GOURD INSTRUMENTS

The instrument at left is clearly a fiddle, complete with a gourd bow and strung with horse hair. The larger instrument is less distinctive; but both were made by Minnie Black of East Bernstadt, Kentucky. It was her contribution to the Bicentennial. Minnie raises all the gourds she uses for making musical instruments and for making a multitude of other items. (Photo by the author)

Hobart Hoskins of Hoskins Hollow on Cow Creek here in Anderson County demonstrates his gourd trumpet which he grew and shaped many years ago. It is on display in the Arnwine Cabin at the Museum. (Photo by Gordon Irwin)

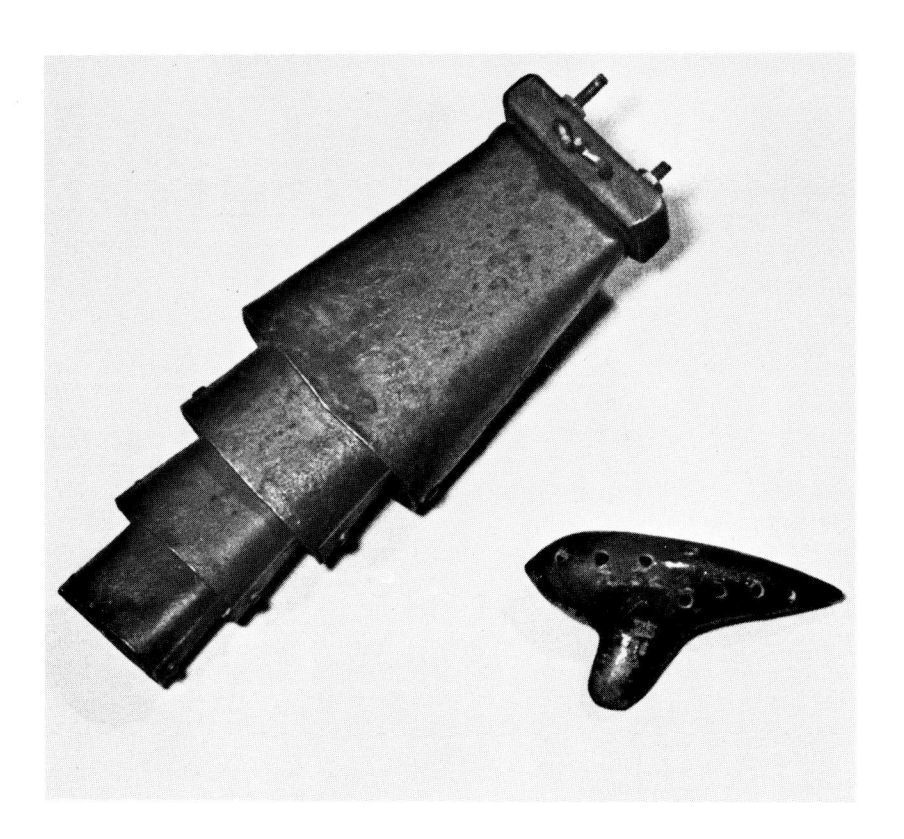

"SWEET POTATO" AND MUSCIAL COW BELLS

This small instrument shown at the right is called a "Sweet Potato" presumably because of its shape. It is the same as an Ocarino. I found it in the attic of the old Johnson house on Clinch River at Kyles Ford in Hancock County, and purchased it about 1970 from Lloyd Johnson, the last occupant of this old homeplace. While the history of the "globular flute" goes back to 2700 years B.C., it became popular around the Civil War period in this country.

These cow and sheep bells are bolted together so that a person may strike either one of the four, thereby creating a higher or lower pitch, depending on the size of the bell. (Photo by Pat and Bill Miller)

JEWS HARPS

The Jews harp, probably correctly the jaws harp, has been played in Europe for hundreds of years, and in Applachia since the first Whites entered the region. The one at top is of recent vintage, the one shown is the center a "turn of the century" Jews harp, and the one pictured on the in the bottom of the photograph dates back to the late 1700's. It was excavated by Gene Purcell at the site of the famous military fort known as Southwest Point, which was located near the present site of Kingston, Tennessee in Roane County. (It is missing the metallic reed.) The music is produced by striking the metal reed, causing a vibration. The pitch is varied by increasing the decreasing the cavity of the mouth. (Photo by the author)

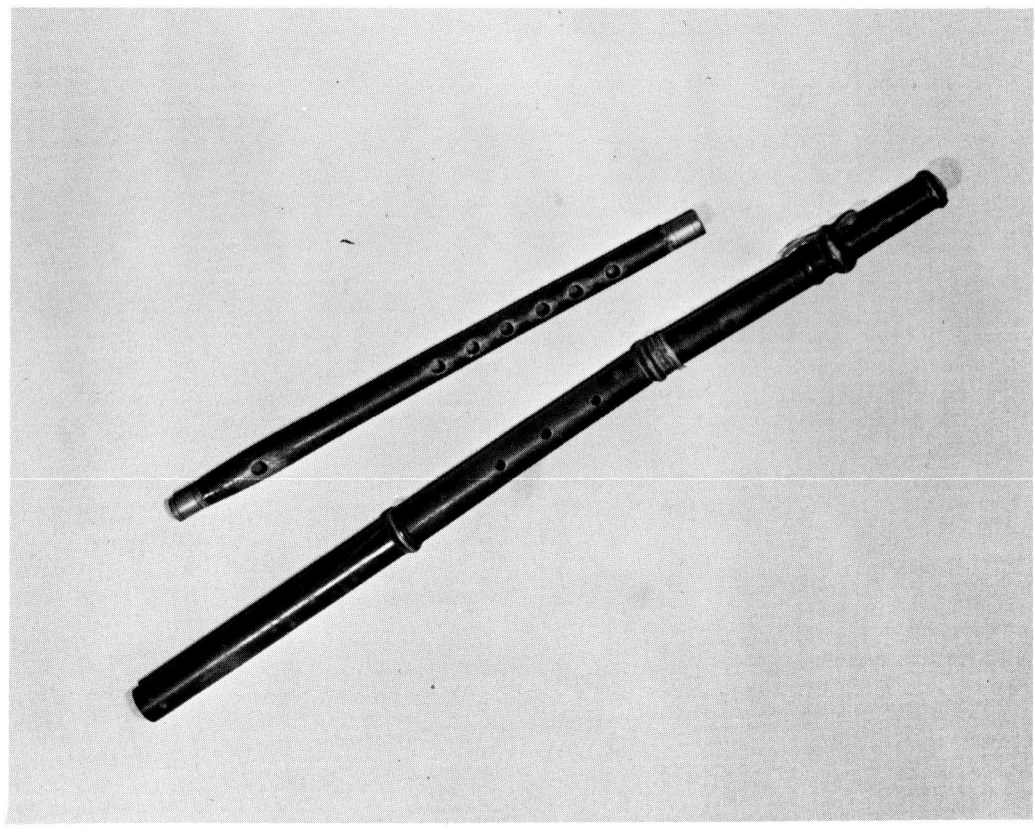

LUTE

Although I doubt it has any Appalachian roots, this instrument is included because it was acquired from an old home in this region. It was purchased about 1964 from Leland Disney who lived several miles west of the Museum in Clinton. It had been in his family for some time, but he did not know its origin. Although the lute was well known in Europe in the 1500's and 1600's, it apparently never "caught on" in this country, especially not in Appalachia. (Photo by Wallace Denny)

CIVIL WAR FIFE AND FLUTE

This old fife, shown at top, was purchased for me by my close friend, W.G. Lenoir, from Tom Rutherford who lived about ten miles north of the Museum in Union County near Big Ridge State Park. It was carried by his father in the Civil War. His father was, I presume by the color of the fife, a Union soldier, as were most all the people in this area.

When I bought the old Sid Meal estate in the village of Clarksburg, seven miles south of Huntington in West Tennessee, this old wind instrument, shown on the right, was discovered. Although I am informed that it is quite old, I have no personal knowledge relative to its history, origin, etc. Family members indicated that it had been there "for as long as we can recollect." (Photo by Pat and Bill Miller)

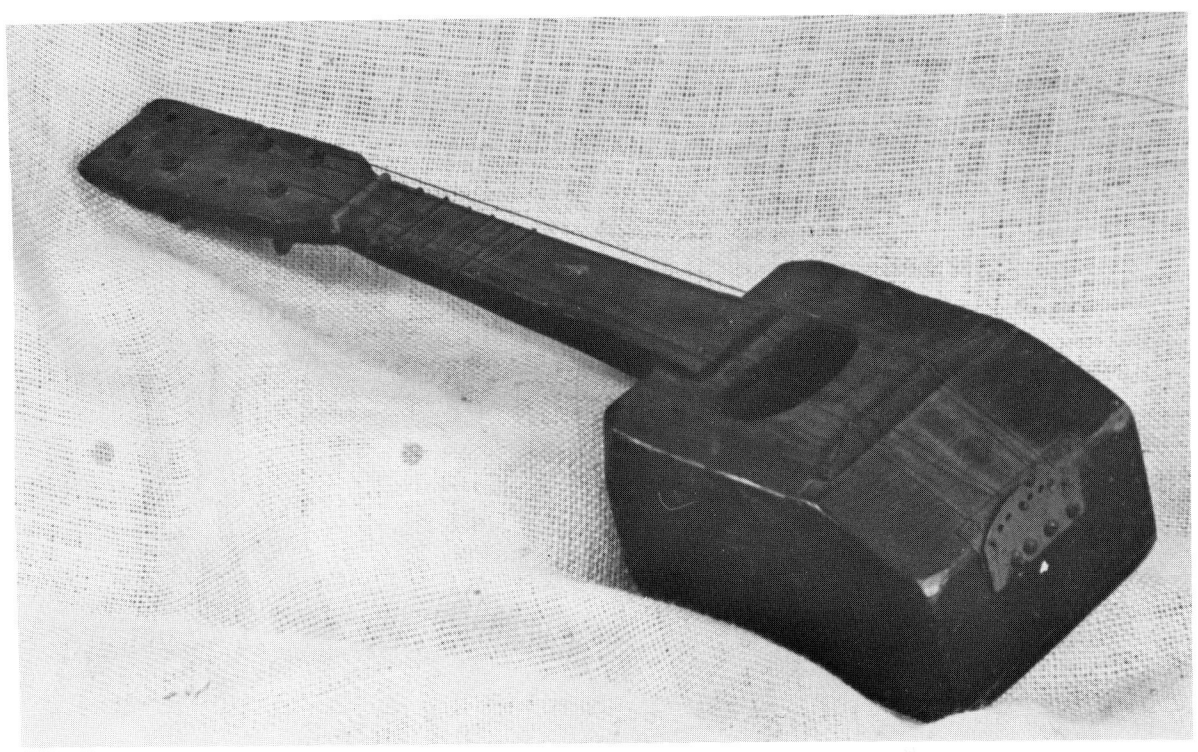

CHEESE BOX MANDOLIN AND FACTORY-MADE "TATER BUG"

The mandolin at top is the only "country" made mandolin I have seen. As stated earlier, the mandolin was seldom even heard of in the mountains until well into the 20th century. This one was acquired from Guy Bowers of Greeneville. He indicated that he bought it in "the old Dutch Settlement" of Greene County, in upper East Tennessee in the 1930's from a man named Pitney Shaw.

It is shown here with the well-made European type mandolin known in this region as a "tater bug" because of the striped, rounded back resembling the Colorado potato beetle, commonly called the potato or "tater bug". In addition to both instruments having eight strings, note other similarities such as the shape of the neck, the sound hole, etc. (Photo by Wallace Denny)

ADDENDUM TO THE FIRST EDITION

Since the completion of *Musical Instruments of the Southern Appalachian Mountains* four years ago, I have acquired a number of most interesting folktype musical instruments, along with pertinent information relative to their origin and history. Rather than reorganize the entire book and insert these photographs and this information in the respective appropriate places, they are being included at the end of the book as an addendum, or a sort of postscript; but with tie-in references made to the proper chapter and topic.

FIDDLE MAKER EVART ACUFF

My longtime friend, the late Evart Acuff, was a native of tiny Union County, Tennessee which produced a number of nationally known early country entertainers such as Chet Atkins, Lois Johnson, Carl Smith and the legendary Roy Acuff. Roy, the undisputed "King of Country Music" and the recent subject of a nationally shown television program in which President Reagan joined in the commendations, is Evart's cousin. Evart and his fiddle making is discussed at some length on pages 13-15; but no pictures were available at the time of the first printing, hence this inclusion. In an interview a short time before his death Evart stated:

"I finished my first one in 1923." "I was carrying the mail in Union County when my great, great uncle Lafayette—called Fate—Cassady gave me his homemade tools he made in his blacksmith shop. I said I could make a fiddle like Uncle Fate had. He said I couldn't, so I did—with some of his help. I've been making them, off and on, ever since."

When Roy Acuff took to fiddling and singing on early radio stations of the area, and dreaming of fame on the Grand Ole Opry, he used one of Evart's instruments. "It's in his museum in Nashville," Evart said.

Evart Acuff is shown working on a fiddle back which he is making from apple wood. (Photo courtesy of Charlie Acuff)

Evart's son Charlie Acuff, a left-handed fiddler, is shown here playing one of the fine instruments his father made. Charlie, who plays at the Museum of Appalachia occassionally, is retired from the Aluminum Company of America and now devotes full time to playing the old fiddle tunes of our ancestors. (Photo by the author)

First Except for the top, this entire instrument, which we shall call a fiddle, is carved from a single piece of pine. The fingerboard portion has been painted black, possibly to simulate the ebony fingerboard of quality violins. A most interesting feature of the instrument is the heavy wear resulting from cording. At one point the wear was so extensive that a wooden patch or rectangular plug has been inserted, and even it is well worn. It originates from the Shenandoah Valley of Virginia, and is now in the Museum of Appalachia collection. (Photo by the author)

Second The inscription inside the body of this most unusual and well-made banjo reads: "Made by F.M. Franklin, April 23, 1932." The top is spruce and the back side and neck are made from maple. I bought it from Roddy Moore who acquired it in Western North Carolina. (Photo by the author)

Third The scroll-shaped neck-terminal of this banjo is the first one I have seen, but I am informed that it was not uncommon in the area where this one was found—at Hillsville, in southwest Virginia a few miles from the North Carolina border. The factory-made head is a recent addition. (Museum of Appalachia collection. Photo by the author)

Fourth The body of this fretless five-string banjo is made from an ordinary tin pan commonly used in the kitchen. I purchased it from trader Mark King who acquired it in Randolph County, North Carolina, near the city of Greensboro. (Museum of Appalachia display. Photo by the author)

THE KINNEY'S AND THEIR HUB CAP BANJO

In the extreme northeastern part of Kentucky, near the Ohio River, live Charles and Noah Kinney who have been making and playing musical instruments since as far back as they can remember. It is only a few miles from the city of Portsmouth, Ohio, about 75 miles east of Cincinnati, and yet it is about as remote and quaint as any section of Southern Appalachia. Charles and Noah live on the ancestral homeplace which can only be reached by a narrow, one-lane dirt road. They both have built modest little houses near the old log home where they were raised; and this old house—filled with parts of homemade banjos and fiddles, serves as a place where they tinker with their instruments, and play the ballads of their ancestors. It was in this old home that I came across the hub cap banjo, which, it seems, adequately represents the ingenuity and imaginativeness of the Kinney's. The head is of tin, the neck of oak, the sides of walnut roughly dressed with a hatchet, and it has three of the gear-type tuners, and two wooden tuning pegs.

The old home also contained a number of almost life-sized, puppet-type dancing men whose strings were controlled by foot pedals so that the Kinney's could have them dance to the music they played. It was for this purpose, and for playing music for their own entertainment, that the hub cap banjo was made.

Noah is shown here at the old Kentucky homeplace, playing the hub cap banjo he made from items he found on the premises and alongside the road.

"We jest gathered up whatever was layin' around and made this here banjo," Noah states. "Hit don't sound too bad when you get it all tuned up." He is shown here with his banjo at the log house where he and Charles grew up. (Photo by the author)

This banjo, like all the instruments made by Charles Kinney and his brother Noah, were made of whatever scrap materials they had or found. The Photograph shows the hub cap used as the resonator. (Photo by Ed Meyer)

Charles Kinney is shown playing the fiddle at the old homeplace near Vanceburg, Kentucky. Although he has made several crude fiddles, starting when he was a boy, this is not one of his make. (Photo by the author)

TOMMY CLINE AND HIS BANJO

Near the foot of the Great Smoky Mountains, and a few miles up Chestnut Creek from the Monroe County community of Ball Play lives Tommy Cline. He is a genuine product of that isolated mountain area—a logger, trapper, wild bee hunter, farmer and piddler. He has built a half dozen tiny buildings and sheds in a narrow hollow above his house, and it was in one of those structures, February 1980, that I encountered this unusual banjo. The head is tanned groundhog hide attached over a rim made from the top of a heavy five-gallon bucket. The head was first laced with string, then held secure by the brackets which are made from a heavy gage wire, each one twisted in the center to create additional tension.

"Now ain't that something", Tommy said when I pulled the banjo from under a pile of old boxes and discarded clothing. "I ain't tried to play him in years—never did play much. They's a feller named Kenneth Williams that made that fer me. He kilt a groundhog, and tanned his hide to make the head with. It ain't doing me no good; so I reckon I'll jest sell him to you fer the Museum so people can see how poor folks had to do." (Photo by the author)

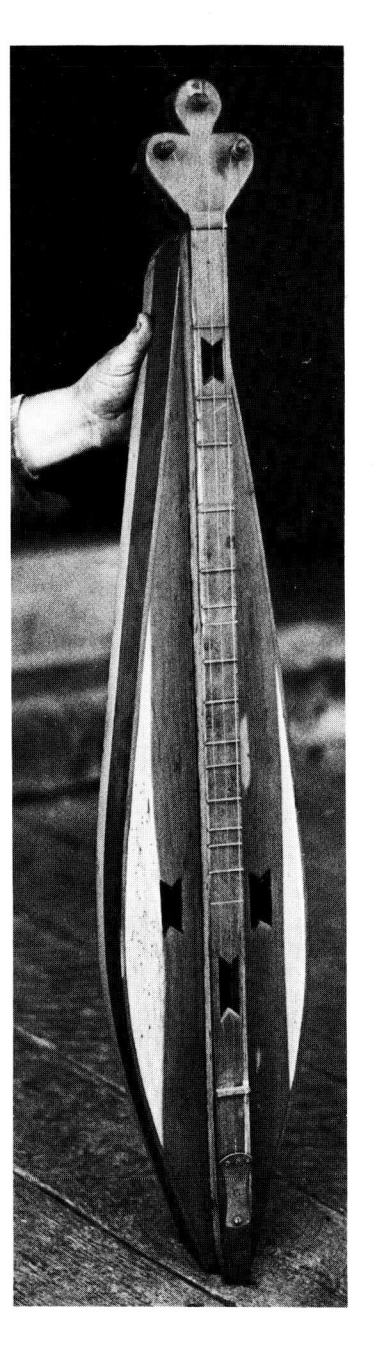

Center This heavy, three string dulcimer made of maple, came from the mountains of western North Carolina, near Ashville. It is 33 inches long, 8 inches wide and 3½ inches in thickness. It's displayed at the Museum of Appalachia. (Photo by the author)

Right Every part of this interesting dulcimer, including the tuning pegs, is made of red cedar. The top, as is the back, is made of a single piece of wood, and the white portion on either side is from the sap portion of the tree.

It was a part of the most extensive Peck Daniels estate, which was sold at public auction about 1979, and Daniels had indicated that this instrument originated in the community of Gray's Station, or Gray, which is located in upper East Tennessee near Jonesboro, the state's oldest town.

The instrument has a total length of 39 inches, a width of 6½ inches at its widest point, and has a depth of 3 inches. It has a clover-type tuning head, a raised, hollow fingerboard, and has three strings. It is a part of the Museum of Appalachia display. (Photo by the author)

Left Because the mandolin was introduced so late into Southern Appalachia, one very seldom finds old hand-made versions. This heavy but well made model has a top of spruce, a back of walnut and mahogany, and a neck of walnut. The intricately carved design in the sound hole may be "S-B-F". The instrument came from the Shenandoah Valley of Virginia and is now at the Museum of Appalachia. (Photo by the author)

97

THE BOX DULCIMER OR SCANTLIN (McNAIRY COUNTY, TENNESSEE)

On a hot day in July 1979, I was purchasing some antiques from an old gentleman named Wilbanks in Montgomery County, Tennessee. As I was leaving I chanced to ask about any old handmade musical instruments and he informed me that his son had an old guitar fitting that description.

When I visited the son, Donald W. Wilbanks, I discovered to my pleasant surprise that the "guitar" was really a rectangular, box-type dulcimer or scantlin, the type which I had known only to exist in two or three countys in the southern part of Middle Tennessee. And sure enough, in response to my querries, Donald informed me that he had found it in an abandoned house in McNairy County (Home of the nationally famous sheriff Buford Pusser, about whom the movie was made). The house from which the instrument came was located near the village of Michie a few miles from the Tennessee River and on the Tennessee-Mississippi state line.

This instrument, slightly over twelve inches in width, is twenty-seven inches in height, three inches deep, and is made of maple, with both the top and back consisting of a single board. It had four strings. Note the five sound holes on each side of the fretboard asymmetrically positioned, two of which are enlarged by mice, or perhaps by one mouse and one rat. (Photo by the author)

This scheitholt, the German type instrument from which the mountain dulcimer evolved, is considered to be a classical transitional piece—more so, dulcimer scholar Ralph Lee Smith believes, that any he has seen. It has the shape and form of the scheitholt, but has the scroll-shaped peg box and other features suggestive of the dulcimer. This unusual instrument originated in Western North Carolina. Smith has photographed a dulcimer which had a peg box and tail piece strikingly similar to the scheitholt shown here. It was, Smith states, made by a wagonmaker family of Mocksville, North Carolina, near Winston-Salem. Perhaps this instrument was made by an older member of that family, or by someone in that area. The cut nails used in construction indicate that this instrument is an early one. It is made of pine, except the peg box which is walnut. It is 39 inches in length, 2½ inches in depth and has a width which varies from 4½ to 2¾ inches. It is on display at the Museum of Appalachia. (Photo by the author)

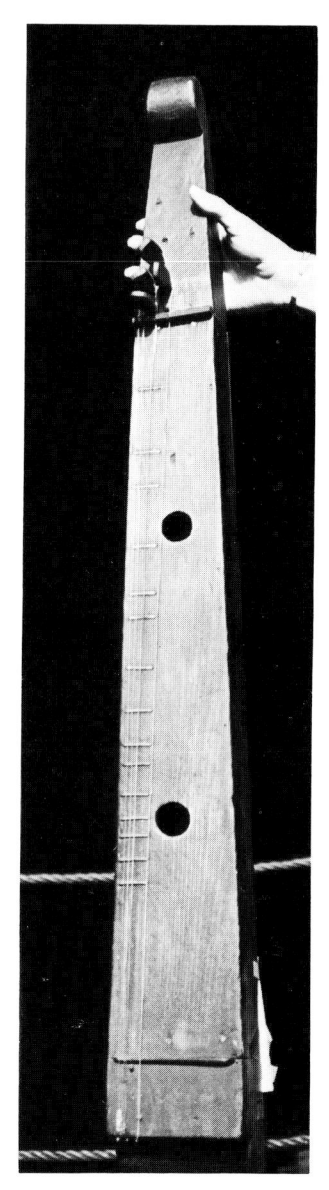

DULCIMER PLAYERS AT PINEVILLE, KENTUCKY

A few years ago the mountain dulcimer was known but to a mere handful of people in isolated spots of Southern Appalachia. Today it is known throughout America and has been enthusiastically adopted by untold thousands, especially the young. This photograph, taken at the dulcimer players workshop at the Pine Mountain State Park near Pineville, Kentucky in 1970 is illustrative of the growing popularity of both the mountain and hammered dulcimer. (Photo courtesy of Ethel Bates)

STEPHEN MELTON DULCIMERS

It is seldom indeed that one finds old dulcimers whose makers' history can be reliably documented. The fact that the maker of these two dulcimers is established, since much is known of his life and domicile, and because of their unusual decorative features, these dulcimers are especially interesting, and historically important. They belong to Ethel Brooks Bates who lives near the village of Gibson Station in Lee County, in the extreme southwestern part of Virginia—about five miles from historic Cumberland Gap. I have found more early dulcimers in Lee County than in any county in Appalachia; and the few scholars who have studied the American mountain dulcimers have, I believe, had similiar experiences.

These instruments were made, according to Ethel, by her grandfather, Stephen Melton, who grew up in the vicinity of Galax, a Virginia town 150 miles east of Gibson Station, near the North Carolina border. Melton, who was a carpenter, came to Lee County when he was about thirty, and settled on a farm near where Ethel now lives. As a small girl she remembers listening to him play the dulcimer, as well as the fiddle, accordion, and banjo. She recalls also that her grandmother thought it was sinful to play the fiddle and banjo, but approved of the dulcimer, possibly because it did not lend itself to dance music.

One of the instrument's shown here was made for his daughter Virginia Melton Brooks (Ethel's mother), and the other he made for another daughter Elizabeth Melton Nevils. The bow which remains in the case with one of the dulcimers, along with Ethel's recollections, confirm that they were played by use of a regular fiddle bow. This is not to say that they were not also played by the plucking method as was most common.

Inasmuch as Stephen Melton died in 1917, and since the dulcimers were made at least a few years before his death, we may assume that they date from the first few years of the century. (Ethel thought they were close to a hundred years old, but that seems a little doubtful.) They are made of pine, have four strings, feature the fully developed scroll peg box, and are decorated by a series of holes both on the front and back.

A back view of Melton's dulcimers showing the tiny "feet" which allows them to be placed on a table, or other solid surface without scratching or damaging the instruments. (Photo by the author)

Ethel Bates with two dulcimers made by her grandfather, Stephen Melton. (Photo by the author)

Said by one noted student of the subject to be the most beautiful dulcimer he had viewed, this instrument was also purchased at the Peck Daniels auction in Bristol, discussed previously. It is one of the very few dulcimers which is signed, presumably by it's maker, J.M. Neff.

Jacob Michael Neff, according to researchers Ralph Lee Smith of Washington, and Professor Roddy Moore of Ferrum, Virginia, lived from 1834 to 1916 in Rural Retreat, Virginia. He reportedly had 13 children, and made a dulcimer for each of them.

The back and front of this lightweight instrument is of pine and the sides, hollow fingerboard, and pegboard are of cherry. It is 34 inches long, 6¾ inches wide at the greatest point, and two inches in thickness. There are no nails, but instead, tiny wooden pegs used in the construction of this dulcimer. It is among the musical instrument display at the Museum of Appalachia and is held by the author's daughter, Elaine Irwin Meyer. (Photo by the author)

The inscription on the back of this dulcimer reads: "J.M. Neff April 20, 1890. It is a raining today". (Photo by the author)

102

INDEX

Acuff, Charles, 14, 92
Acuff, Evart, 13, 14, 15, 18, 92
Acuff, Roy, 9, 13, 14, 15, 18, 92
Allred, Florence, 19, 85
Amati, 13
Atkins, Chet, 8, 9, 13
Atkins, Frank, 83
Autry, Gene, 9
Baker, Sen. Howard, 28, 59
Banjo, 13, 31-58
Barnett, Maw, 76, 80
Bates, Ethel Brooks, 100, 101
Bays, Thad, 76
Bean, Carl, 8, 17, 27
Bell, Noah, 53
Black, Minnie, 68, 88
Blackwell, Earl, 58
Blevins, Charlie, 35
Boone, Daniel, 80, 82
Bowers, Guy, 20, 22, 57, 80, 82, 91
Brewer, Alberta, 77
Brewer, Carson, 77
Brooks, Hugh, 73
Brooks, Virginia Melton, 100
Bunch, Tyler, 59, 62
Butler, Carl, 9
Butler, Pearl, 9
Byrd, David, 23, 81
Campbell, Archie, 9, 83
Campbell, Linnie, 87
Campbell, Sherman, 50
Carlisle, Bill, 9
Carrico, John, 31, 67
Carrico, Mrs. John, 67
Carson, Fiddlin' John, 13, 83
Carter Family, 31, 83
Carter, "Mother" Maybelle, 83
Carter, President, 9
Cassady, A.L., 13, 14, 15, 18
Cassady, Fate, 92
Cassady, Richard, 14

Cassady, Tom, 18
Children's Museum of Oak Ridge, 28
Cline, Tommy, 96
Coffman Family, 34
Collins, Levi, 33
Combs, Josaih H., 65
Costa, Mary, 9
Couch, Frank, 17
Country Music Hall of Fame, 11, 19, 32, 44, 50, 53, 69, 76
Cox, Bob, 8, 12, 18, 83
Cox, Clyde, 25
Crawford, Victory, 46
Crockett, Davy, 29
Crosby, Powell H., 78
Cross, Hugh, 9, 10
Crowell, Bob, 41
Daniels, Peck, 97, 102
Disney, Leland, 90
Dulcimer, 64-82
Duncan, Rep. John, 28
Eledge, Kellie, 49
Eledge, Rufus, 49
Elliott, Tate, 52
Ely, 76
Fiddle, 13-30
Fife, 90
Flatt, Lester, 9
Flatt and Scruggs, 9
Flute, 90
Ford, Tennesse Ernie, 9
Gallahars, 25
Gardner, Bob, 10
Glandon, Esco, 86
Glen, Chris, 56
Godwin, Hazel, 71
Grand Ole Opry, 13, 14, 15, 16, 31, 83
Grant, General, 51
Graves, Grant, 39
Graves, Luther, 38
Graves, Rufus, 38

Graves, Scott, 38
Greene, Jack, 9
Guitar, 83, 85, 86, 87
Harmonica, 83
Harris, Homer, 87
Hay, Judge George, 13
Hill, Lee, 43, 44, 58, 85
Hill, Luther, 19, 85
Hodges, Shirley Crosby, 78
Holley, James T., 78
Holley, W.T., 78
Homer and Jethro, 9
Horner, Charles Gene, 16, 17
Hoskins, Hobert, 88
Houndshell, Vestie, 70
Idol Family, 34
Irwin, Glenn, 12
Irwin, Grandfather, 72
Irwin, Lee, 15
Jefferson, Thomas, 31
Jews Harp, 12, 83, 89
Johnnie and Jack, 9
Johnson, Bob, 27
Johnson, Elisha, 51
Johnson, George Allen, 73
Johnson, Lloyd, 89
Johnson, Lois, 9, 13
Johnson, "Tater Hole" Joe, 45
Kelley, Harrison, 25
Kinch, Charles, 21
King, Mark, 36, 93
King, Ray, 55, 66, 87
Kinney, Charles, 94, 95
Kinney, Noah, 94, 95
Koch, Ed, 9
Lambert, Stillman, 26
Lambdin, Chuck, 61
Leinarts, 25
Lenoir, W.G., 59, 90
Lute, 90
Mac and Bob, 10

INDEX

Macon, Uncle Dave, 31
Mandolin, 83, 91
Martin, Asa, 83
Martin, Rowe, 29
Maxwell, John, 69
McCarroll, Fiddlin' Jimmy, 10, 17, 84
McCarroll, George, 17
McCoy, Worth, 24
McFarland, Lester, 10
McKinnie, Walter, 10
McLain, John, 23, 81
McNeeley, Larry, 9
Meal, Sid, 90
Melton, Stephen, 100
Meyer, Elaine Irwin, 102
Monroe, Bill, 9, 12, 31, 83
Moore, Charles R., 13
Moore, Grace, 9
Moore, Roddy, 26, 45, 48, 72, 75, 102
Morton, Reba, 67
Mouth Bow, 59-63
Mullins, Bill, 70
Mullins, Burchett, 53
Mullins, Dora, 70
Mullins, Earl, 70
Mullins, Howard, 53
Murphy, Michael, 64
Museum of Appalachia, 6, 7, 8, 10, 11, 12, 24, 26, 30, 32, 33, 42, 44, 52, 58, 59, 63, 64, 74, 83, 86, 88, 90
Music Box, 84
Neff, Jacob Michael, 102
Novelty Hawaiians, 10, 30
Ollis, Harry Lee, 41
Paganini, 13
Parky, Andy, 17
Parton, Dolly, 9
Peer, Ralph, 83
Pollard, Dr., 82
Presley, Elvis, 87

Presnell, Ed, 77
Puckett, Riley, 9
Pugh, Dow, 42
Purcell, Gene, 89
Pusser, Buford, 98
Queen Victoria, 31
Reagan, President, 92
Rice, Grandfather, 38
Ritchie, Jean, 65
Roane County Ramblers, 10, 84
Robertson, Andrew J., 78
Rogers, "Happy Jack", 8
Rogers, Horney, 4
Rogers, Roy, 9
Russell, Jim, 84
Rutherford, Tom, 90
Ryan, Paul, 46, 47, 81
Schilling, Jean, 77
Schilling, Lee, 77
Scruggs, Earl, 9, 31
Sievers, Fiddlin' Bill, 10, 30
Sievers, Mack, 10, 30
Sievers, Willie, 10, 30
Sharp, Don, 38
Sharp, Hiram, 28, 29, 47, 59, 63
Shaw, Pitney, 91
Skillet Lickers, 9
Smiths, 25
Smith, Carl, 9, 13
Smith, Professor J. Allen, 64, 72
Smith, Ralph Lee, 64, 98, 102
Speaks, Willie, 70
Stewart, Alex, 59, 60, 61, 62
Stewart, Boyd, 61
Stooksbury, Amos, 83
Stooksbury, Carlock, 8, 12
Stooksbury, Eli, 59, 61
Stradivari, 13
Sutton, Bob, 53
Sweeney, Joel Walker, 31

"Sweet Potato", 89
Swor, Sallie, 74
Syck, Allen, 44
Taylor, Alf, 57
Taylor, Bob, 13, 57, 83
Taylor, Jerry, 30
Tennessee Ramblers, 10, 30
Thompson, Jimmy, 13
Tinch, Jim, 56
Tinch, Thurman, 54, 55, 56
Vincent, Bert, 45
Walker, Cas, 9
Walker, Mary Ellen, 40, 74
Walton, Nancy, 29
Ward, Don, 75
Warren, Ruby, 72
Warwick, Lawrence, 59, 61, 63
Wayland, Jack, 57
Weems, Robert, 69
Welch, Arthur, 34
Wells, Kitty, 9
Whitaker, Renda, 32
White, Bonnie, 81
White, Sam, 81
Wilbanks, Donald W., 98
Williams, Billy, 49
Williams, Kenneth, 96
Wink, Pat, 51
Wolfe, Charles K., 10, 30, 64, 83
Wyrick, Ted, 8